W9-CFZ-384

COMMUNICATING WITH
GRAMMAR
Skills for Life

Silvija Kalnins
Jaklin Zayat

OXFORD

UNIVERSITY PRESS

OXFORD
UNIVERSITY PRESS

Oxford University Press is a department of the University of Oxford.
It furthers the University's objective of excellence in research, scholarship,
and education by publishing worldwide. Oxford is a registered trade mark of
Oxford University Press in the UK and in certain other countries.

Published in Canada by
Oxford University Press
8 Sampson Mews, Suite 204,
Don Mills, Ontario M3C 0H5 Canada

www.oupcanada.com

Library and Archives Canada Cataloguing in Publication

Kalnins, Silvija, author
Communicating with grammar : skills for life. 2 / Silvija Kalnins
& Jaklin Zayat.

ISBN 978-0-19-900333-4

1. English language—Grammar.   2. English language—Textbooks for
second language learners.   I. Zayat, Jaklin, author   II. Title.

PE1112.K34 2014   428.2'4   C2012-905796-7

Cover image: © Rubens Abboud/Alamy

Printed and bound in Canada

1 2 3 4 — 17 16 15 14

Authors

Silvija Kalnins, BA, CTESL, has been teaching and coordinating English for the past 10 years at La Cité collégiale. This is her third career. As the eldest daughter of Latvian immigrants, she has experienced first-hand the difficulties of English language acquisition, which has sensitized her to the needs and challenges that her students face.

Jaklin Zayat, BA (Modern Languages), M.Ed., has been teaching ESL and academic writing for over 20 years. She speaks five languages and is recognized for her knowledge of the construction of many other languages. She currently teaches at La Cité collégiale and the University of Ottawa. A co-author of *Famous Canadian Authors*, she also enjoys writing stories for future publications.

Series Team

The whole author team created the approach, the topics covered, and the chapter structure for the three-level series *Communicating with Grammar: Skills for Life*. Though each level has its specific lead author or authors, the team worked collaboratively in the development of these publications.

Alice Johnston-Newman, BA, MA, CTESL, is a language teacher, writer, and translator with close to 30 years' experience teaching English as a first and second language to Canadians, new Canadians, and international students. She is currently a professor at La Cité collégiale in Ottawa and has taught at Algonquin College, Carleton University, and abroad. During her professional career, she has created and adapted teaching material and student workbooks for ESL, enriched level, as well as specialized, career-oriented English courses.

Mohammad Hashemi, BA, MA, is a teacher, editor, translator, and author. He has been coordinating and teaching English for more than 20 years, formerly at Carleton University and Algonquin College. He currently teaches at La Cité collégiale in Ottawa, Ontario. For more information about Mohammad visit his website at www.mohammadhashemi.com.

Julita Milewski, BA, M.Ed., has been an ESL teacher for the last 13 years. Her desire to teach ESL started as she herself was learning English as a second language when she first immigrated to Canada as a teenager. Her teaching experience includes working with adolescent and adult learners, international students, and immigrants. She has taught at the University of Ottawa, Carleton University, and various private language schools. She is currently an ESL professor at La Cité collégiale in Ottawa.

Acknowledgements

From the Authors

We thank our families and friends for their understanding and patience from the beginning to the end of this project. We thank our colleagues too for their support and encouragement during this amazing journey. Our students should be specially thanked for their suggestions and ideas when we tested our grammar exercises in class. With the support and encouragement of all our team members for Levels 1 and 3 of the CWG series, we finally see the fruits of our labour, aided by the unfailing assistance and professional advice of the editorial and publishing team at OUP Canada.

Reviewers

Oxford University Press Canada would like to express appreciation to the instructors and coordinators who graciously offered feedback on *Communicating with Grammar* at various stages of the developmental process. Their feedback was instrumental in helping to shape and refine the series.

Gill Atkinson	Camosun College
Roisin Dewart	Université du Québec à Montréal
Susan Drolet	Cégep Garneau
Barbara Fraser	Collège Ahuntsic
Daniela Geremia	
Brandie Glasgow-Spanos	Niagara Catholic District School Board: St. Ann Adult Learning Centre
Emrah Görgülü	Simon Fraser University
Therese Gormley Hirmer	Humber College Institute of Technology & Advanced Learning
Kristina Gryz	Red River College
Corinne Hamel-Taylor	S.U.C.C.E.S.S.
Eva Ing	George Brown College
Rob Inouye	Simon Fraser University
Maureen Kelbert	Vancouver Community College
Kristibeth Kelly	Fanshawe College
Kara King-Barratt	Catholic Crosscultural Services
Izabella Kojic-Sabo	University of Windsor
Claire La Fleur	The Centre for Skills Development & Training
Anita Lemonis	Vancouver Community College
Sandra Madigan	Southeast Regional College
Corinne Marshall	Fanshawe College
Lara McInnis	Humber College
Jennifer Peachey	VanWest College
Mark Rankin	
Brett Reynolds	Humber College
Cheri Rohloff	The University of Winnipeg
Wilfried Schuster	Toronto District School Board: Adult Ed
Adrianna Semerjian	City Adult Learning Centre
Marti Sevier	Simon Fraser University

CONTENTS

Introduction ix

PART 1

Chapter 1
Simple Present and Present Progressive 1

Simple Present 2
Present Progressive 8
Bringing It All Together 12
Chapter Review 17

Chapter 2
Nouns and Pronouns 21

Nouns 22
Pronouns 27
Bringing It All Together 32
Chapter Review 37

Chapter 3
Articles and Determiners 41

Articles 42
Determiners 44
Bringing It All Together 52
Chapter Review 57

Chapter 4
Simple Past, Past Progressive, *Used to*   59

Simple Past   60
Past Progressive   64
Used to   68
Bringing It All Together   70
Chapter Review   76

Chapter 5
Comparatives, Superlatives, and Equatives   79

Comparative and Superlative Adjectives   80
Comparative and Superlative Adverbs   85
Equatives   89
Bringing It All Together   91
Chapter Review   94

Chapter 6
The Future   99

The Future Using *Will*   101
The Future Using *Be Going To*   106
Expressing the Future with the Simple Present Tense   109
Expressing the Future with the Present Progressive Tense   111
Bringing It All Together   113
Chapter Review   117

Part 1 Review
Self-Study   121

PART 2

Chapter 7
Combining Clauses   129

Coordinating Conjunctions   130
Conjunctive Adverbs in Compound Sentences   132
Relative Pronouns as Conjunctions   134
Indefinite Pronouns and Adjective Clauses   136

Subordinating Conjunctions in Complex Sentences 139
Bringing It All Together 141
Chapter Review 146

Chapter 8
Present Perfect 149

Present Perfect: Indefinite or Unspecified Past 150
Present Perfect: Past to Present 154
Present Perfect: Repeated Past Actions 158
Bringing It All Together 160
Chapter Review 165

Chapter 9
Modals 169

Modals Expressing Ability 171
Modals Expressing Necessity or Obligation 173
Modals for Giving Advice and Making Suggestions 175
Modals for Making Polite Requests and Asking Permission 178
Modals for Showing Present and Future Possibility 180
Bringing It All Together 183
Chapter Review 186

Chapter 10
Types of Questions and Short Answers 189

Yes / No (Interrogative) Questions 190
Negative Questions 193
Information Questions 196
Tag Questions 199
Bringing It All Together 202
Chapter Review 206

Chapter 11
Prepositions and Phrasal Verbs 209

Prepositions of Time 210
Prepositions of Place 212
Phrasal Verbs Part 1 214
Phrasal Verbs Part 2 (Separable and Non-separable verbs) 218
Bringing It All Together 220
Chapter Review 225

Chapter 12
Past Perfect and Conditionals   227

    Past Perfect   228
    Conditionals   232
    Bringing It All Together   238
    Chapter Review   242

Part 2 Review
Self-Study   245

Appendices   253

    Appendix A: Common Irregular Verbs   253
    Appendix B: Conjunctive Adverbs   255
    Appendix C: Subordinating Conjunctions   256
    Appendix D: Phrasal Verbs   257

Glossary   259

INTRODUCTION

Welcome to *Communicating with Grammar*!

Communicating with Grammar: Skills for Life is a Canadian series for ESL and EFL students looking to improve their understanding of English grammar. Offering grammar instruction through the use of the four skills—reading, writing, listening, and speaking—the series helps students internalize concepts for better use in all their communication. Students improve their command of English grammar through a broad spectrum of activities that set them up for further study or work in an English-speaking environment.

The *Communicating with Grammar* series employs a task-based and communicative methodology. Using a "learn–practise–use in context" approach, the books deliver the essential grammar concepts via practical exercises and activities, helping learners become functional in English as quickly and efficiently as possible. The communicative activities then help students internalize the grammar in context.

Series Features

This Canadian series guides student learning by combining a communicative task-based approach with discrete grammar instruction using traditional exercises. It provides warm-up activities, explicit grammar teaching, considerable use of practical example sentences, and a combination of mechanical and interactive exercises. The more traditional exercises allow students to practise each concept, while engaging communicative activities further reinforce the grammar being studied. Moreover, the target grammar is embedded in the reading, listening, and writing sections that follow, facilitating further grammar use in context. Additionally, review units provide, at regular intervals, an opportunity for students to practise the material and solidify the key aspects of their learning. The books have the additional advantage of providing flexibility for those learners who thrive on extra challenge while maintaining the intended level of the target material.

Chapter Structure

Chapters are logically organized into an overview, a series of grammar topics with practice, a cumulative section incorporating all four skill areas, and a summary. Grammar is treated as a necessary component of all four skill areas, and students are encouraged to use the focal grammar topic with each of these skills in every chapter.

Overview

Each chapter opens with a very brief explanation of the chapter's grammar topic, followed by a **Warm-up** activity that engages students and provides an opportunity to start thinking about and using the target grammar in context. Given a real-life task, students are encouraged to use the new grammar concept to communicate with their classmates.

Grammar

The chapter's target grammar is divided into logical and manageable parts, each of which uses a learn–practice–use in context approach.

The grammar instruction starts with a **Formation** (learn) section that offers a clear explanation of the grammar topic, often by using tables and charts, and illustrates the mechanics in context.

Exercises (practice) follow the grammar explanation. A series of traditional drills gives students controlled exposure to the language structures and deals with common difficulties faced by most learners. The exercises are varied and include sentence completion, sentence construction, matching, ordering, error correction, transformation, multiple choice, fill in the blanks, and more.

Further practice through interactive **Communicative Activities** (use in context) allows students to apply the new grammar topic in a practical manner. These engaging tasks, which include class, pair, and group activities, enable learners to communicate in an authentic way by using the grammar they have learned.

Bringing It All Together

This key section at the heart of the chapter provides an opportunity for students to bring together all the chapter's grammar parts and apply them in a more authentic context. It includes a number of additional **Communicative Activities** that challenge students to incorporate all aspects of the chapter's grammar. The **Reading** section contains both a reading passage and comprehension questions, requiring students to apply the chapter's grammar points. The audio clips and comprehension questions in the **Listening** section again facilitate input and output of the target grammatical structures. In the **Writing** section, students are provided with another productive opportunity to apply the grammar, this time in a longer piece of writing.

Chapter Review

Each chapter's review section opens with a helpful **Summary** of all aspects of the grammar taught in the chapter; students can check their learning through a complete and convenient chapter grammar reference. The traditional **Exercises** that follow are designed to give additional straightforward practice for students to work on independently in class or for homework.

Appendices and Glossary

To supplement and support the learning, each book ends with quick-reference appendices, with additional information on grammar points or usage, and a glossary of all key vocabulary from the chapters' Readings.

Three Levels

Level 1 is designed for students with basic English who still need to build a solid foundation of the major verb tenses and sentence structure. Students learn to formulate more accurate sentences and questions through the grammar lessons and exercises. They expand their English vocabulary through the Reading and Listening components. This level also focuses on targeting the common basic grammatical errors students may still need to learn how to correct.

Level 2 is designed for students who have completed Level 1 or who have enough grammar and a basic understanding of the four skills to formulate questions in English and construct more-complex sentences. At the entry into this level, students can usually clearly communicate their intentions to others but still make frequent errors in structure, tense, and usage that may slow comprehension. Level 2 focuses on improving grammar in the four skills areas to an exit level at which students will have more fluency, a larger vocabulary, and the ability to express themselves by using more complicated sentence structures.

Level 3 is the bridging level to fluency in English usage. This level completes all the perfect verb tenses and has chapters on the active and passive voice and reported speech. It further develops students' ability to construct more-complex sentences with the study of clauses. Reading and Listening components are from authentic sources, preparing students for real-world communication. At the completion of this level, students will have the confidence to communicate with native speakers academically or professionally.

Additional Series Components

- Class audio is available for each level in the series. It contains either authentic or constructed listening clips, depending on the level and grammar topic.
- The **online Teacher Resource** contains teaching notes and aids, additional communicative activities and exercises to be used as practice or in a test setting, audio transcripts, and an answer key for the exercises and the reading and listening comprehension questions.

PART 1

1 SIMPLE PRESENT AND PRESENT PROGRESSIVE

2 NOUNS AND PRONOUNS

3 ARTICLES AND DETERMINERS

4 SIMPLE PAST, PAST PROGRESSIVE, *USED TO*

5 COMPARATIVES, SUPERLATIVES, AND EQUATIVES

6 THE FUTURE

1 Simple Present and Present Progressive

OVERVIEW

The simple present and the present progressive are the first two verb tenses that second-language learners see.

- We use the simple present to talk about facts, habits, or routines:

    The sky is blue.

    I swim every day.

    We go grocery shopping on Saturdays.

- The present progressive is a two-word verb: the present tense of the verb *be* + the present participle (base + *-ing*). We use the present progressive to talk about things that are happening at this moment, or at this point in time:

    This week we are studying English verbs.

    I am talking to my students.

    The children are playing in the park.

SIMPLE PRESENT

Warm-up

Frequency adverbs tell how often something happens. Some examples are *never*, *sometimes*, or *always*. With a partner, match the frequency adverbs in Column 2 with those in Column 1 that mean the same.

1. seldom
2. sometimes
3. often
4. usually

a. frequently
b. generally
c. rarely
d. occasionally

With a partner, add each of the following words to the table, in the correct place.

seldom   generally
often   rarely
usually   occasionally
frequently

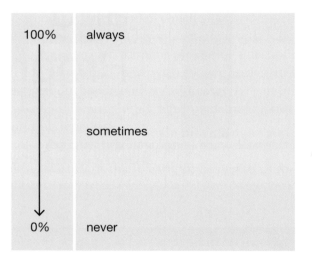

Work in pairs. Discuss your routine and habits for getting ready to go out in the morning, Monday to Friday. Use either an adverb of frequency from above, or an expression of frequency. Here is one routine to get you started:

get up → I get up every day at 6:00 AM.

| every day | each week | twice a week | three times a week |

Formation

Positive Statement (one-word verb)	Yes / No Question	Wh- (Information) Question	Negative Statement
I **walk**.	**Do** I **walk**?	Where **do** I **walk**?	I **do not walk**.
You **walk**.	**Do** you **walk**?	Where **do** you **walk**?	You **do not walk**.
He / She / It **walks**.	**Does** he / she / it **walk**?	Where **does** he / she / it **walk**?	He / She / It **does not walk**.
We **walk**.	**Do** we **walk**?	Where **do** we **walk**?	We **do not walk**.
You **walk**.	**Do** you **walk**?	Where **do** you **walk**?	You **do not walk**.
They **walk**.	**Do** they **walk**?	Where **do** they **walk**?	They **do not walk**.

- The simple present describes facts and habits.
- Positive statements have a one-word verb.
- The third-person singular (*he*, *she*, *it*) of the simple present ends in -*s*.
- Questions and negative statements need the auxiliary *do*:

    I **do**   you **do**   he / she / it **does**   we **do**   you **do**   they **do**

- Wh- questions (also called information questions) use keywords: adverbs and expressions of frequency.
- Negative statements can use contractions:

    do not → don't   does not → doesn't

SPELLING RULES FOR SIMPLE PRESENT VERBS

- Most forms of simple present verbs (with the exception of *be*) are the same, other than the third-person singular:

I cook	We cook
You cook	You cook
He / She cook**s**	They cook

- When forming the third-person singular, an *s* is generally added to the base form of the verb.
- Add -*es* to verbs ending in *s*, *sh*, *ch*, *o*, or *x*:

    wish → wish**es**   watch → watch**es**   go → go**es**   fix → fix**es**

- Change *y* to *ie* and add -*s* for verbs ending in consonant + *y*:

    marry → marr**ies**   study → stud**ies**

- For verbs ending in a vowel + *y* keep the *y* and add -*s*:

    play → play**s**   stay → stay**s**

EXERCISE 1

Fill in the blanks to correctly complete the sentences. Use the words from the list. Use each word only once. Look at the example to help you.

~~swim~~	open	drive	watch	go	pay	write	read	study

He _____ swims _____ every day before class.

1. Anne _____ television every evening after dinner.

2. The gym _____ at 9:00 AM and closes at 10:00 PM every day.

3. I usually _____ to school because the bus is often late.

4. Adam is a good student. He _____ for three hours every night.

5. My grandparents don't use email. They always _____ letters.

6. Do your parents _____ your tuition fees?

7. How many books do you _____ each month?

8. Steve works for a British company. He _____ to London twice a year.

EXERCISE 2

Change each of the following sentences into a yes / no question.

He swims every day before class. → Does he swim every day before class?

1. They play basketball on Saturdays.

   _____?

2. I usually go to the library after class.

   _____?

3. He often travels overseas on business.

   _____?

4. She always has a burger and fries for lunch.

   _____?

5. We go skiing every winter.

   _____?

ADVERBS OF FREQUENCY

When using the simple present to describe habits or routine, we often use adverbs of frequency with the verb.

always	often	rarely	three times a week
usually	sometimes	hardly ever	twice a month
generally	occasionally	never	each week
frequently	seldom	every day	

Their placement within sentences follows patterns.

1. After the verb *be*:

   She is always late.

   Carlos is often absent on Mondays.

   I am usually in class at 9 AM.

2. Before all other verbs:

   They often eat in the cafeteria.

   I hardly ever drink coffee at night.

   Anna rarely wears dresses or skirts.

3. After the subject in yes / no and wh- (information) questions:

   Does he often go to the movies?

   Why do they rarely use public transit?

   Do you usually sleep on long plane journeys?

4. Phrases related to days, weeks, months, seasons, and years come at the end of the sentence or question:

> Sam has eggs for breakfast every day.

> I put gas in my car three times a week.

> Do they go camping every summer?

EXERCISE 3

Fill in the blanks with the best adverb of frequency for each of these sentences.

1. Christina is _____ (always / never / hardly ever) tired after school, so she goes to bed early.

2. Bill and Margaret are _____ (generally / occasionally / never) at home in January. They go on vacation every January.

3. Sophie _____ (sometimes / rarely / every week) buys ice cream after soccer practice. Her favourite flavour is strawberry.

4. You should take your dog for a walk _____ (seldom / three times a day / each year).

5. We _____ (always / never / occasionally) go to a concert on Saturday nights, but we also like to stay at home.

6. Do you _____ (never / every day / generally) take your lunch to work, or do you go to a restaurant?

7. Does Sebastian win the English prize _____ (always / every term / hardly ever)?

8. I _____ (often / frequently / rarely) eat meat; I eat a mostly vegetarian diet.

Wh- (Information) Questions

Question Word	To Ask for Information About . . .	Example Sentences
who	a person	Who does she want to see?
what	a thing	What do you want?
where	a place	Where does he go for lunch?
when	time	When does the train arrive?
why	a reason	Why is she late?
how	method or degree (often used in expressions such as *how far*, *how many*, *how often*, *how long*)	How do they train for a marathon? How do you make sushi? How does she work and study full-time? How hot is the soup? How long is the movie? How often do you call your mother?

We use wh- questions (also called information questions) when we need specific information. When forming a wh- question, remember to use the appropriate question word for the type of information you want to find out.

EXERCISE 4

Change each of the following sentences to a wh- (information) question. Look at the **bolded**, underlined words. What kind of information do they give (who, what, where, when, why, or how)? Use this information to choose the correct question word.

They want to see the teacher **after class.** → When do they want to see the teacher?

1. They live **in an apartment**.

   _____?

2. He has an 8:00 class **every day**.

   _____?

3. She meets with **her tutor** twice a week.

   _____?

4. My son drives **his car** only on the weekends.

   _____?

5. He is absent today **because he has a driving test**.

   _____?

6. A soccer game is **90 minutes** long.

   _____?

EXERCISE 5

Change each of the following positive sentences into the negative.

Julie wants to eat at the mall. → Julie does not (doesn't) want to eat at the mall.

1. I play the piano very well.

   _____

2. You need to renew your passport every year.

   _____

3. Sandra usually organizes the neighbourhood barbecue.

   _____

4. Paul goes fishing every Sunday afternoon.

   _____

5. The children always brush their teeth before bed.

   _____

6. We need an extra week to finish this assignment.

   _____

SUBJECT QUESTIONS

Subject questions ask about the subject of a sentence. The sentence structure is the same as the structure of a positive statement, with the wh- (information) question word (*who, what, which, how much, how many*) replacing the subject.

Statement	Subject Question
My sister wants to go to British Columbia. **My brother** plays the guitar in the band.	**Who** wants to go to British Columbia? **Who** plays the guitar in the band?
Smoking is not permitted in the restaurant. **A baseball game** is on television tonight.	**What** is not permitted in the restaurant? **What** is on television tonight?
Ten centimetres of rain usually falls in June. **A lot** of information is on the Internet. **Eight hours** of sleep every night is healthy.	**How much** rain usually falls in June? **How much** information is on the Internet? **How much** sleep is healthy?
Twelve students want extra help. **Two** slices of pizza are left. **Twenty** people need tickets to the play.	**How many** students want extra help? **How many** slices of pizza are left? **How many** people need tickets to the play?
This book about the environment is interesting. **The World Cup** takes place every four years.	**Which book** is interesting? **Which sports event** takes place every four years?

EXERCISE 6

Change each of the following sentences to a wh- (information) question. The information you want to ask about is **bolded** and underlined. Use the words from the list. Each word may be used more than once.

who	what	which	how much	how many

<u>**Susan**</u> is knocking on the door. → <u>**Who**</u> is knocking on the door?

1. **The fruit** is on the delivery truck.

   _____?

2. **These** shoes are very expensive.

   _____?

3. **My son** runs marathons.

   _____?

4. The laptop **on the shelf** is for sale.

   _____?

5. **All** of the furniture in the store is on sale.

   _____?

6. The jewellery **in the showcase** is very beautiful.

   _____?

7. **Several** children are not at school.

   _____?

8. The dogs **in the park** are very playful.

   _____?

9. **Six** bikes are missing from inventory.

   _____?

10. **Professor Wilson** teaches Advanced Computer Science.

   _____?

PRESENT PROGRESSIVE

Warm-up

Work in pairs. Look at the photo and discuss what is happening at this college. You may want to use these:

now   this semester
right now   this week
at this moment

Formation

The present progressive tense is formed using the present tense of the verb *be* + present participle (base + *-ing*).

Positive Statement	Yes / No Question	Wh- (Information) Question	Negative Statement
I **am playing**.	**Am** I **playing**?	Where **am** I **playing**?	I **am not playing**.
You **are playing**.	**Are** you **playing**?	Where **are** you **playing**?	You **are not playing**.
He / She / It **is playing**.	**Is** he / she / it **playing**?	Where **is** he / she / it **playing**?	He / She / It **is not playing**.
We **are playing**.	**Are** we **playing**?	Where **are** we **playing**?	We **are not playing**.
You **are playing**.	**Are** you **playing**?	Where **are** you **playing**?	You **are not playing**.
They **are playing**.	**Are** they **playing**?	Where **are** they **playing**?	They **are not playing**.

EXERCISE 7

Fill in the blank with an appropriate verb of your choice. Remember to make the verb agree with the subject.

Julien _____ the exam right now. → Julien **is writing** the exam right now.

1. The students _____ the video right now.

2. The teacher _____ the exams this week.

3. The children _____ the museum this semester.

4. Look! It _____ outside.

5. People _____ their cars very slowly and carefully.

EXERCISE 8

Write yes / no questions using information from the sentences in Exercise 7.

Is Julien writing the exam right now?

1. _____?

2. _____?

3. _____?

4. _____?

5. _____?

EXERCISE 9

Change each of the following sentences to a wh- (information) question. Look at the **bolded**, underlined words. What kind of information do they give (who, what, where, when, why, or how)? Use this information to choose the correct wh- word. You may want to refer to the Question Words chart on page 5.

Heidi is taking <u>**an English class**</u> this term. → What **class** is she taking this term?

1. She is going <u>**to her classroom on the second floor**</u> right now.

   _____?

2. Now, she is buying <u>**her books**</u> at the bookstore.

   _____?

3. <u>**Her classmate Rachel**</u> is helping her to find the cafeteria.

   _____?

4. She is meeting her teacher <u>**after lunch**</u> for extra help.

   _____?

5. She is listening to an English conversation <u>**on her laptop**</u>.

   _____?

6. Heidi is happy <u>**because she is speaking English**</u>!

   _____?

EXERCISE 10

Fill in the blanks to correctly complete the sentences. Use the words from the list. Remember to make the verb agree with the subject. There may be more than one correct answer. Look at the example to help you.

~~listen to~~	watch	win	lose	have	organize	plan	make	cook

She _____ to her sister sing. → She **is listening** to her sister sing.

1. Students _____ problems accessing the wireless network today.

2. The school basketball teams _____ all of their games this semester.

3. The students' association _____ a fundraiser.

4. His mother _____ his lunch this semester.

5. We _____ a video in class this week.

EXERCISE 11

On a separate piece of paper, write negative statements using information from the completed sentences in Exercise 10.

She is not (isn't) listening to her sister sing.

STATIVE VERBS

Stative verbs express emotions, thoughts, beliefs, and knowledge. We do not generally use these verbs in the present progressive.

Emotions	Thoughts and Beliefs	Knowledge
want She wants a new cellphone. I want to go home.	**think** I think it's dinner time. I think the assignment is due on Monday.	**know** I don't know his email address. Catherine, do you know Thomas?
need I need a new winter coat. You need to pay your rent.	**believe** Do you believe in ghosts? You can pass this course. I believe in you!	**understand** We never understand his lectures.
like, love I like Chinese food. They love their new house.	**trust** Do you trust your country's politicians? She is quite sick, but she trusts her doctors.	**remember** I never remember people's names. My friend always remembers my birthday.
prefer Do you prefer tea or coffee? Does he prefer to use a laptop or a tablet?		**forget** I always forget to water my plants! Don't forget to feed the dog.
hate I hate the traffic at rush hour. She hates getting up early.		
mind I don't mind pizza, but I prefer pasta. Do you mind if I sit here?		
hope I hope she likes me. I hope I'll pass this course.		

1. The verb *think* can be used in the present progressive when you are talking about the action of thinking:

   What do you think we should do? BUT

   You're very quiet. What are you thinking about?

   Continued

2. In conversation, it is becoming more common to hear verbs of emotion (especially *love*, *like*, *hope*, and *want*) expressed with the present continuous. This is not required, but it emphasizes that the speaker is feeling the emotion *now*, rather than in a general sense:

> I love chocolate ice cream. (= a general emotion)
>
> I am loving my new office space. (= a current emotion)
>
> I hate science courses. (= a general emotion)
>
> I am taking a science course right now, and I'm hating it. (= a current emotion)

EXERCISE 12

Fill in the blanks with the correct tense of the verbs in parentheses.

1. Usually I _____ (wear / am wearing) contact lenses, but today I _____ (wear / am wearing) glasses.

2. _____ (Are you preferring / Do you prefer) skiing or skating?

3. Ben rarely _____ (cooks / is cooking) dinner, but tonight he _____ (makes / is making) chicken curry.

4. Sarah _____ (takes / is taking) a math class this year, but she _____ (hates / is hating) it.

5. I always feed my neighbours' cat when they _____ (go / are going) on vacation. They _____ (trust / are trusting) me.

6. You _____ (need / are needing) new boots for the winter.

7. I _____ (don't mind / am not minding) flying, but I _____ (prefer / am preferring) to take the train.

8. You _____ (don't listen / are not listening) to the teacher. What _____ (do you think / are you thinking) about?

BRINGING IT ALL TOGETHER

COMMUNICATIVE ACTIVITY 1

Getting to Know You

Make a chart like the one on the next page. Work with a partner. Ask your partner about his or her activities. How often does your partner do the things in the chart? Put a check mark (✓) in the correct place in the chart. You can also ask about one or two of your own ideas. Then, write a short paragraph about your partner. Remember to use the simple present tense.

My partner, Julie, swims every morning from Monday to Friday. After her swim, she showers, eats her breakfast, and gets ready for school. She takes the bus to school every day at 9:00 AM and arrives at 9:30 AM. She frequently studies her English on the bus. She often drinks a coffee before class.

Habit	Never	Occasionally	Frequently	Always
exercise				
drink coffee				
study English				
take the bus				

COMMUNICATIVE ACTIVITY 2

What's Up?

Now find a new partner. Look at the chart below showing some keywords. Discuss the school semester using the keywords given and the present progressive tense. Complete the chart. Now, with this information, write about your partner's semester using complete sentences.

Right now Robert is thinking about his timetable. He has a lot of homework this week. He is taking seven courses this semester. Today he is writing a paper for his English class. He is also doing some research for a History essay. However, he is making some exciting plans for the weekend!

Keywords	Right Now	Today	This Week	This Semester
English class				
homework				
courses				
timetable				
research				
plans				

✂ COMMUNICATIVE ACTIVITY 3

Look at the pictures. Can you find 10 differences?

1. _____   6. _____

2. _____   7. _____

3. _____   8. _____

4. _____   9. _____

5. _____   10. _____

Reading

Read the passage and answer the questions that follow.

ENGLISH AT AN EARLY AGE: EUROPEAN CHILDREN DISCOVER THE WORLD OF ENGLISH

"Happy birthday to you!" Johann, age four, is singing in English. He also knows the days of the week, and he can count to 10. Johann lives in Switzerland, a country with four <u>official</u> languages, but he is learning English as his second language—and he loves it.

A major change is taking place across Europe, and Johann is part of that change. Johann's first language is German, and his country's other official languages are French, Italian, and Romansch, but he is not learning those languages. His parents think English is more important. Johann and

his three-year-old sister go to private English classes twice a week. Parents all over Europe are making the same choice for their children, and private English education is growing quickly. Children in these countries often learn English in primary school, but parents often believe an early start is better.

Studies show that these parents might be right. Early <u>bilingualism</u> helps students to learn a third or fourth language easily in high school or university. Some <u>researchers</u> think bilingualism helps children to <u>achieve</u> higher grades in school.

For Europe's schoolchildren, learning English is different from learning any other foreign language. Children can listen to pop songs, watch television, or play Internet games in English every day. These sources provide <u>support</u> and <u>encouragement</u> to children like Johann.

Official government policy is not always so helpful. Some countries are trying to pass laws to limit the spread of English; they want to protect their national language. However, these laws are rarely <u>effective</u> and they are often difficult to <u>enforce</u>. The use of English is growing steadily all over Europe, as more and more children like Johann enter English classes every year.

COMPREHENSION

Answer the following questions. Use complete sentences.

1. What is happening in many countries in Europe?

   _____

   _____

2. How does bilingualism help children in their future studies?

   _____

   _____

3. For Europe's schoolchildren, why is learning English different from learning any other language?

   _____

   _____

4. What are some countries doing to limit the spread of English?

   _____

   _____

5. The children in this reading are ages four and three. Do you think that this is a good age to begin learning a second language? Why, or why not?

   _____

   _____

Listening

🔊 *Track 1*

STUDENT LIFE

Listen to the audio.

COMPREHENSION

Answer the following questions. Use complete sentences.

1. What English course is Emily taking this semester?

   _____

2. How many courses is Jonathan taking this semester?

   _____

3. When is Jonathan graduating?

   _____

4. When does Jonathan work?

   _____

5. What night is Jonathan free?

   _____

6. Where does Emily work?

   _____

7. When does Emily study?

   _____

8. Who is Emily going to the gym with?

   _____

Writing

Write a short composition (150 words) about ONE of the following topics:

What is your favourite subject? Why do you like that subject? Are you taking a course in your favourite subject right now? If yes, are you enjoying it? Why? If no, what courses are you taking? Are you enjoying them?

Do you play on a sports team? What position do you play? Why do you like your sport? Is your team having a successful year? Why, or why not?

Summary

- The simple present is used to describe facts, habits, or routines.

- Most forms of simple present verbs (with the exception of *be*) are the same, other than the third-person singular, where an *-s* is usually added to the base form in the third-person singular.

- When using the simple present to describe habits or routine, adverbs of frequency are often used.

- The present progressive is used to describe ongoing action at the present time.

- Stative verbs are verbs that express emotions, thoughts, beliefs, and knowledge. These verbs are used in the present progressive only when the speaker wishes to emphasize that the emotion is felt *now*.

EXERCISE 1

Rewrite the following passage. Change the second person (*you*) to the third-person singular (*he* or *she*). Make all the necessary changes to pronouns and verbs.

> You are a student. → He is a student.

You are a student. You live in a house with three friends. Every day, you walk to school. This year, you are studying business management at the college and you are doing very well.

_____

_____

_____

EXERCISE 2

Fill in the blanks with the correct tense of each verb in parentheses. Use either the simple present (*make*) or the present progressive (*am making*).

1. There _____ (**be**) twenty people in the room.

2. Everyone _____ (**work**) hard right now.

3. Every Friday morning, the teacher _____ (**give**) the students a quiz.

4. This morning, the students _____ (**do**) a quiz on verb tenses.

5. Most of the time, the students _____ (take) only five minutes to do the quizzes.

EXERCISE 3

Change each of the following statements to a yes / no question.

I have two cats. → Do you / I have two cats?

1. Félix enjoys playing soccer.

   _____?

2. Anna and Chloë are going to the gym.

   _____?

3. They don't want to go to the movies.

   _____?

4. He is talking to the class about his experience.

   _____?

5. Jean wants to drive his car to the party.

   _____?

EXERCISE 4

Change each of the following sentences to a wh- (information) question. The information you want to ask about is **bolded** and underlined.

Karl wants to eat lunch <u>later</u>. → When does Karl want to eat lunch?

1. She is **<u>running a marathon</u>** right now.

   _____?

2. He flies to Calgary **<u>once a week</u>**.

   _____?

3. The children play **<u>in the park</u>** after lunch.

   _____?

4. They understand **<u>the grammar lesson</u>** better now.

   _____?

5. The girls are waiting for **their mother** right now.

   _____?

EXERCISE 5

Change each of the following positive sentences into the negative.

   The dogs are barking in the house. → The dogs **are not** (**aren't**) barking in the house.

1. The students are taking food into the language lab.

   _____

2. His mother is waiting at the bus stop.

   _____

3. The president of the college interviews students once a week.

   _____

4. She takes the train in the morning.

   _____

5. He texts his girlfriend every hour.

   _____

EXERCISE 6

Change each of the following statements into subject questions. The information you want to ask about is **bolded** and underlined.

1. **Karl** loves his two dogs.

   _____?

2. The homework **from today's class** looks interesting.

   _____?

3. **Several** tables in the cafeteria are dirty.

   _____?

4. **The ceiling fans** aren't working well.

   _____?

5. **Very little** advice is available about travel in this country.

   _____?

EXERCISE 7

Fill in the blanks using either the simple present or the present progressive tense. Pay attention to key words in the surrounding text as this will give you a clue as to the appropriate verb tense to use.

Alan _____ (take) seven courses this semester. His program, Travel and

Tourism, _____ (be) two years long. He _____ (enjoy)

his courses this semester but he _____ (have) a lot of homework.

He _____ (find) this difficult as he also _____ (have)

a part-time job. This week he _____ (change) his schedule. His

alarm _____ (ring) at 6:00 AM. He _____ (finish) his

homework before he _____ (go) to school. He now _____

(have) time after class to take a nap before he _____ (go) to work. He

_____ (work) at a restaurant close to the school so he usually walks,

but today he _____ (drive) his car.

EXERCISE 8

There are seven verb tense errors in the following paragraph. Find and correct them.

Look! It begins to rain. Unfortunately, I am not having my umbrella with me. It is

in my car. Leslie is being fortunate because she wears a rain jacket. It rains quite

hard. We are having to wait for the bus but there is not being a bus shelter.

Nouns and Pronouns

PART 1

1 SIMPLE PRESENT AND PRESENT PROGRESSIVE

2 NOUNS AND PRONOUNS

3 ARTICLES AND DETERMINERS

4 SIMPLE PAST, PAST PROGRESSIVE, *USED TO*

5 COMPARATIVES, SUPERLATIVES, AND EQUATIVES

6 THE FUTURE

OVERVIEW

- Nouns are words for people, places, or things.
- Nouns can be proper, common, abstract, or collective.
- Nouns are either countable (you can count them) or non-countable (you can't count them).
- Pronouns replace nouns.
- Pronouns can be personal, possessive, reflexive, indefinite, demonstrative, or relative.

Warm-up

Work with a partner. Your teacher will give you some cards. Choose one of your cards, but don't show your partner. Describe the word on your card. You must not say the word! Your partner will try to guess the word.

You: This is something you eat on a special day. It is sweet. It tastes good.

Your partner: Hamburger!

You: No . . . remember, it's sweet. It has candles on the top.

Your partner: Birthday cake!

You: Yes, that's right!

NOUNS

A noun is a word for a person, a place, an object, or an idea. Nouns can be proper, common, abstract, or collective. They can also be countable or non-countable.

Warm-up

Fill in the chart with your favourite people, places, and things.

	Person	Place	Thing
1	Lady Gaga		
2		Hawaii	
3			chocolate
4			
5			

Share your favourites with your group.

PROPER, COMMON, ABSTRACT, OR COLLECTIVE?

Formation

- Proper nouns refer to recognized names of people or places and they always have a capital letter.

  Justin Trudeau, President Obama, Canada, July, Saturday

- Common nouns refer to any one of an entire category of people or objects.

    child, toy, pen, day, nurse, house

- Common nouns take the indefinite article *a* or *an*. They can also take the definite article *the*.

- Some proper nouns and many common nouns can be pluralized.

    There are five **Saturdays** this month.

    Mondays are my hardest **days**.

    The **prime ministers** of the G8 **countries** held a meeting.

- Abstract nouns refer to an idea, feeling, belief, or concept.

    Good **health** is very valuable.

    Love makes the world go round.

    I believe in using **fairness** to decide.

    They wanted **equality** for all people, men and women alike.

- Collective nouns are singular nouns that refer to groups of people.

    Our city's hockey **team** just won the Stanley Cup!

    The **committee** decided to have a meeting to decide on how to organize the plan.

EXERCISE 1

<u>Underline</u> the nouns in the following paragraph. The first one has been done for you.

I'm very excited about my travel <u>plans</u>! I am going to South America for three weeks with my soccer team. We plan to teach soccer skills to young children in a poor village. I want to pack my bags right now. I need two pairs of shorts and three T-shirts. It's cool in the evenings, so I need a sweatshirt, too. And, of course, I need my soccer boots and some thick socks. Health is very important, so I mustn't forget my vitamins and sunscreen. The whole group is excited about this trip. I know we'll see some poverty, but I hope we can have fun with the children. I'll miss my family, but I can't wait to go!

EXERCISE 2

Work in pairs. Look at the picture. How many proper, common, abstract, and collective nouns can you find in the picture? Fill in the chart on the following page.

	Proper	Common	Abstract	Collective
1				
2				
3				
4				
5				

PLURALS OF NOUNS

If the noun ends in a consonant or a silent *e*, add -*s*.

  program → program<u>s</u>   place → place<u>s</u>

If the noun ends in *s*, *sh*, *ch*, *o**, or *x*, add -*es* to form the plural.

  bus → bus<u>es</u>   tomato → tomato<u>es</u>
  box → box<u>es</u>   sandwich → sandwich<u>es</u>
  soccer match → soccer match<u>es</u>

Some common exceptions: kilo → kilos, photo → photos, piano → pianos, and radio → radios.

If the noun ends in a **consonant + y**, change *y* to *ie* and add -*s*.

  strawberry → strawberr<u>ies</u>
  candy → cand<u>ies</u>   party → part<u>ies</u>

If the noun ends in a **vowel + y**, keep the *y* and add -*s*.

  day → day<u>s</u>   toy → toy<u>s</u>

Remember: when the subject is singular, the verb is singular, and when the subject is plural, the verb is plural.

  People are waiting.

People is plural and the verb *are* is plural.

  Everyone is here.

Everyone is singular and the verb *is* is singular.

  Be careful with the following nouns:

1. Collective nouns—for example, *team*, *group*, *family*, and *committee*. These usually take a singular verb:

    The team **has** decided to practise two days a week.

    The group **meets** at 7:00 PM every Wednesday.

2. Nouns that follow *each* and *every*. These nouns are treated as singular nouns:

    Each day **brings** lots of new experiences.

    Every player **is** working hard.

There are many irregular plurals in English.

Singular	Plural	Singular	Plural	Singular	Plural
child	children	foot	feet	sheep	sheep
woman	women	tooth	teeth	curriculum	curricula
man	men	leaf	leaves	moose	moose
mouse	mice	life	lives	knife	knives
goose	geese	person	people	wife	wives

EXERCISE 3

Fill in the blanks with the correct plural form for the nouns in the following paragraph.

All the child___ at this summer camp have many toy___ to play with: they have five toy car___, two toy bus___, three doll___, and five board game___. They also have lots of snack___ to eat: they each have five chocolate bar___, four bag___ of candy___, potato chip___, and assorted nut___. The camp supervisor___ always encourage the kid___ to eat more fruit___, like apple___ and banana___, instead of candy___ .

EXERCISE 4

Are the following sentences correct or incorrect? If a sentence is correct, write a check mark (✓). If a sentence is incorrect, correct the mistake.

1. How many books do I need for this course? _____

2. I would like some potatos with my steak. _____

3. Can you pass me those boxes? _____

4. Who are those guys at the bus stop? _____

5. Oh no! There are mice in my house! _____

6. The dentist wants to take out two of her tooths. _____

⁂ COMMUNICATIVE ACTIVITY 1

Volunteer Voyagers

Work in groups of three. You are all members of a team or group. You are going to another country to do volunteer work. Work together to plan your trip. Think about the questions below.

- What kind of team or group are you?
- Where are you going?
- Why are you going there?
- What do you need to take?
- What must you not forget?
- Is there anything you are worried about?
- What do you hope to learn on this trip?

Share your ideas with the class.

COUNTABLE OR NON-COUNTABLE?

Formation

Countable nouns are those that can be counted. Examples are *cup, dog, computer, desk, jacket,* and *bus.* These nouns have plural forms.

Non-countable nouns cannot be counted. They do not have plural forms. These fall into the following groups:

- **Abstract nouns.** We cannot touch these. Examples are *news, information, advice, happiness, poverty, equality, fun, knowledge, luck, beauty, health.*
- **Common nouns (categories).** These include *furniture, luggage, money, homework, machinery, software, music, weather.*
- **Common nouns (mass nouns).** These are substances such as *oil, sand, toothpaste, perfume, paint, mud.*
- **Food items.** Examples are *coffee, tea, milk, sugar, rice, bread, cheese, pasta, wine.* Note that some food items can be used as countable nouns, especially when ordering food in a restaurant.

  I'd like some coffee, please. (non-countable)

  Can we have three coffees, please? (countable)

- **School subjects.** Examples are *mathematics, statistics, politics, geography, history.* Note that those words ending in -s are treated as singular nouns.

Some words exist only in the plural form; there is no singular form. Some examples are *scissors, jeans, shorts, glasses, congratulations.*

EXERCISE 5

Fill in the blanks to correctly complete the sentences. Use each word from the list once.

history	rice	oil	luggage	toothpaste	advice	news	software

1. Don't forget to change the _____ in your car.

2. Carla needs new _____ for her trip to Mexico.

3. We have good _____ for you. We want to offer you the job.

4. Can I use your _____? I want to brush my teeth.

5. David wants to design a house on his computer, but he doesn't have the right _____.

6. The Chinese restaurant on the corner serves really good fried _____.

7. I want to improve my English. Can you give me some _____?

8. Zarina's favourite subject is _____. She likes learning about the past.

EXERCISE 6

Fill in the blanks with the correct form of the words in parentheses.

1. There are two _____ (man) at the door. Who are they?

2. I feel tired this morning. I need lots of _____ (coffee).

3. Today, more _____ (woman) are working in high-paying jobs.

4. Vicky is eating salad for lunch. She wants to lose 10 _____ (kilo).

5. These _____ (cabinet) and _____ (dresser) are really old. We need some new _____ (furniture).

PRONOUNS

Pronouns can be personal, demonstrative, and indefinite.

Formation

PERSONAL PRONOUNS

Personal pronouns are used to replace nouns and their modifiers. They can be subject, object, possessive, and reflexive.

Subject Pronoun	Object Pronoun	Example Sentences
I	me	**I** wrote lots of essays. The teacher helped **me** with my essay. Why didn't you tell the joke to **me** too?
you	you	**You** are late again. I am sending **you** to the principal's office. I asked **you** a question.
he	him	**He** is here. I like **him**; **he**'s a nice person. I gave a present to **him** on his birthday.
she	her	**She** wants some coffee. Let's invite **her** to lunch. We promised **her** a new computer.

Continued

Subject Pronoun	Object Pronoun	Example Sentences
it	it	Is the goldfish dead? **It** isn't moving. I have an extra handout. Do you need **it**? Please give **it** some food.
we	us	**We** eat at noon. Why don't you meet **us** in the cafeteria? Can you show the secret passage to **us**?
you	you	Do **you** all like candy? I miss **you** all so much! Let me tell **you** a story.
they	them	Bill and Amy have their coats on. **They** want to leave. Can you drive **them** to the station? Let's throw a party for **them**.

DEMONSTRATIVE PRONOUNS

Demonstrative pronouns are words that replace nouns by indicating specifically whether they are close or far.

Singular Demonstrative Pronoun	Plural Demonstrative Pronoun
this	these
that	those

This replaces a person, place, or thing that is close to the speaker or writer. *This* can also replace a person, place, or thing when the listener or reader knows to what or to whom you are referring.

> **This** book is too expensive.

> **This** restaurant looks good. Let's eat here.

The plural of *this* is *these*.

> **These** oranges look delicious.

> **That** book is a required text in my Economics class.

> **That** neighbourhood is nice, but it's really expensive.

The plural of *that* is *those*.

> **Those** snow-capped mountains over there are very high.

POSSESSIVE PRONOUNS AND REFLEXIVE PRONOUNS

Each personal pronoun has a corresponding

- possessive adjective (*my, your, his, her, its, our, their*)
- possessive pronoun (*mine, yours, his, hers, its, our, yours, theirs*)
- reflexive pronoun (*myself, yourself, him/herself, itself, ourselves, yourselves, themselves*)

We use a possessive pronoun to replace a possessive adjective and its noun.

This is **my book.** It is **mine.**

We use reflexive pronouns to make clear that we did something alone, without any help. Usually we are proud of the action.

This is my new motorcycle. I bought it **myself.**

I love your sweater! Did you make it **yourself?**

We don't need a mechanic. We can fix the car **ourselves.**

Note that we sometimes also use reflexive pronouns with actions that we do *to* ourselves; this is usually related to the human body.

I fell on the ice and hurt **myself.**

Can your baby feed **himself?**

Be careful with the knife; don't cut **yourself.**

Personal Pronoun	Possessive Adjective	Possessive Pronoun	Reflexive Pronoun	Example Sentences
I	my	mine	myself	That is **my** cellphone. It is **mine.** I paid for it **myself.**
you	your	yours	yourself	The hamburger is **your** order. It is **yours.** You ordered it **yourself.**
he	his	his	himself	**His** key is here. This key is **his.** He opened the door **himself.**
she	her	hers	herself	**Her** picture is beautiful. That picture is **hers.** She painted the picture **herself.**
it	its		itself	The puppy ran away from **its** new house. The puppy found the house **itself.**
we	our	ours	ourselves	**Our** new apartment is on the tenth floor. The tenth floor apartment is **ours.** We decorated it **ourselves.**

Continued

Personal Pronoun	Possessive Adjective	Possessive Pronoun	Reflexive Pronoun	Example Sentences
you (plural)	your	yours	yourselves	Is this **your** new baby? Our baby is six months old. How old is **yours**? Do you make his baby food **yourselves**?
they	their	theirs	themselves	Is **their** car the white one? No, the black car is **theirs**. Nice car! Did they buy it **themselves**?

EXERCISE 7

Tarzan, the famous man of the jungle, was brought up by apes and learned English from the human travellers who crossed his path. Some of these travellers were also not native English speakers. Many spoke without using pronouns.

Below is a description of Tarzan's life. Replace each **bolded**, underlined word with the correct third-person subject pronoun, object pronoun, possessive pronoun, or reflexive pronoun.

<u>Tarzan</u> likes to eat bananas. → <u>He</u> likes to eat bananas.

Tarzan is a good man living in the jungle. Mother ape and father ape raised **Tarzan**. Mother ape taught **Tarzan** to take care of **Tarzan** (reflexive) and **mother ape** showed Tarzan how to find food. Father ape taught Tarzan how to survive in the jungle and also taught **Tarzan** how to fight other dangerous animals in the jungle.

Tarzan lives in a big tree house that **Tarzan** built by **Tarzan** (reflexive). Tarzan considers **Tarzan's** tree house as **Tarzan's** castle. The tree house has a bedroom with a large hammock for a bed and a kitchen where **Tarzan** cooks delicious tropical meals.

Tarzan wondered why **Tarzan** looked different from other apes. Tarzan thought that **Tarzan** was very alone until one day **Tarzan** met other human beings.

At first **Tarzan** was very happy to meet others like **Tarzan** (reflexive), but human beings were not all very nice. **Human beings** were not always kind to other animals. Sometimes the humans killed other animals for no reason. Tarzan cried many times when **Tarzan** saw this. These humans didn't cry at all for the animals. Sometimes Tarzan was very sad, but the animals kept **Tarzan** happy. One day Tarzan saw a beautiful female human being. **Tarzan** asked the woman's name. **The woman** said, "My name is Jane." So Tarzan introduced **Tarzan** (reflexive). They fell in love.

Tarzan and Jane are very happy in the jungle. Sometimes Jane goes away to the city to see her family. Tarzan misses **Jane** when she is far away.

When Jane comes back, Tarzan is very happy. **Tarzan** jumps up and down and makes noises like an ape.

Tarzan likes the gifts that Jane brings when **Jane** comes back. **Jane** brings strange food and clothing. **Jane** also brings papers and books with pictures and scribbles. Jane is teaching Tarzan to read and **Tarzan** is teaching **Jane** to hunt and to climb trees. **Jane and Tarzan** are very happy, and soon **Jane and Tarzan** will have a baby. The baby will be called Boy.

EXERCISE 8

For each sentence, fill in the blank with the correct pronoun in parentheses.

1. He always does his homework _____ (himself / hisself / itself); his parents never help him.

2. _____ (Us / We / Ourselves) would like to come and visit you next spring.

3. Jane and _____ (I / me / my) are good friends.

4. I don't need any help, thanks. I can do it _____ (yourself / mine / myself).

5. You can't sit at this table. This table is _____ (ourselves / ours / our).

6. The children should be careful with the scissors. They might cut _____ (theirselves / themself / themselves).

7. Whose laptop is this? It isn't _____ (my / me / mine). Is it _____ (yours / your / you)?

8. Annie and Marc, this cake is wonderful! Did you make it _____ (yourself / yourselves / themselves)?

INDEFINITE PRONOUNS

Indefinite pronouns are used for people and things.

People	Things
someone, somebody, everyone, everybody, anybody, anyone, nobody	something, nothing, anything
Someone is knocking at the door.	**Something** is crawling over her foot.
Anyone can come to the party.	**Anything** you say is hard to hear.
Everyone is invited.	**Nothing** he does surprises me.
Nobody came to visit me.	

Someone is knocking at the door.

This means that a person is doing the action. We assume it is one person and we don't know who it is.

Nobody came to visit me.

Nobody here means not even one person came. It is indefinite because it is not clear whom we are talking about. It is very general.

Remember: All these indefinite pronouns ALWAYS take a singular verb.

Everyone <u>is</u> here.

Everybody <u>is</u> using this app. (*Is* is a singular verb)

Everyone <u>has</u> a copy of the brochure. (*Has* is a singular verb)

EXERCISE 9

Fill in the blanks with the correct indefinite pronouns.

1. _____ is possible.

2. _____ is impossible.

3. For thousands of years _____ only dreamed of flying.

4. They tried _____, from attaching giant wings to their arms to jumping off cliffs with strange suits.

5. _____ is enjoying the advancement of technology.

6. _____ likes the abuse of technology these days.

7. Is there _____ else we can dream about?

8. Is there _____ who dreams of time travel?

9. Could _____ ever believe that these types of dreams come true?

10. Others believe that _____ can happen when you're doing dangerous stunts.

BRINGING IT ALL TOGETHER

COMMUNICATIVE ACTIVITY 2

Guessing Game

Divide into groups of four. Within each group, form two teams.

Team A: Write on a piece of paper the name of a celebrity. Fold the paper and place it in the middle of the table.

Team B: You have to guess the name of the celebrity. You can ask only 10 questions. Use pronouns in your questions.

Is the person a man?

Is *he* an actor?

Does *she* act in movies?

Then switch roles. Continue guessing music groups (use *they*), and then famous movies (use *it*).

COMMUNICATIVE ACTIVITY 3

Who Owns the Puppy?

Jill is a photographer. Today she is taking a photo of a family on this street, but she has a problem. She can't remember which number the family lives at. She remembers that the family has a puppy. Jill meets some neighbours in the street, and they give her information about the five families.

Your teacher will give you cards numbered from 1 to 14. Use the information on each card to fill in the boxes below. Who owns the puppy? Which house should Jill go to?

Number	Country	Family Members	Job	Hobby	Pet
1.					
2.					
3.					
4.					
5.					

COMMUNICATIVE ACTIVITY 4

Dice Game

Work in groups of three or four. Your teacher will give you a die. Throw the die. Look at the number you get, and answer that question. Share your experiences with your classmates.

1. How important is health in your life? What do you do to stay healthy? If you could choose between perfect health and great wealth, which would you choose?

2. What was the best restaurant meal you have ever had? Where did you have it? What did you eat? What did you drink? Who were you with? How expensive was it?

3. Tell us about a time when you had to do something difficult, and you had no help. What was the task? Did you do it yourself? How did you feel afterwards?

4. Tell us about a time when you hurt yourself. What did you do? Did you go to the hospital or the doctor? When did you feel better?

5. Tell us about a time when you met someone very interesting. Who was the person? What did you talk about? Did the person tell you anything surprising?

6. Imagine you are in your house, at night. No one else is home. You hear a strange sound coming from your attic. What do you do?

Reading

Read the passage and answer the questions that follow.

THE ATTIC

"Can I go up to the <u>attic</u>, Mom?" I asked my mother on many occasions, but the answer was always the same. "No, darling; not now. When you get older, we'll go up together and I'll show you what's up there."

Growing up, I had to learn <u>patience</u>, but my older brother Ty (his name is actually Tyrone) didn't make it easy. He was named after the actor Tyrone Power because my father liked his movies, but we always call him Ty. He always makes fun of me wanting to go up to the attic. He always says, "Why do you want to go up there, silly? There are ghosts up there, you know!" Or sometimes he will run up to me and lie about a family meeting about the attic, when there is no such thing.

Well, today I'm 17. Yesterday, Mom and Dad left for Quebec City for the week and they left me in charge of the house. Ty is a year older than I am, but somehow I'm in charge. I have the keys to the <u>cellar</u>, the garage, the shed, and, yes, the attic.

"'Bye . . . enjoy your week! Don't worry about a thing," I shouted as they pulled out of the driveway yesterday. My heart was racing. The <u>adrenaline rush</u> of finally finding out what is in that secret attic was killing me. As they say, "<u>Curiosity</u> killed the cat," but I'm going to take a deep breath and take it easy.

I have waited one full day and now I can't wait anymore. It's 3:00 PM. Ty is at soccer practice. I'm going up to the attic. I have to tell you about our house first. It's a three-, maybe four-hundred-year-old house in Montreal. Many of the homes on our street are remodelled, but they have the old structure. In order for me to go up there, I have to unlock a big door, go up the stairs, and then unlock another smaller door. The doors are thick and heavy. The lock on them still takes an old-fashioned big metal key and the key hole is <u>withered</u> and worn off a bit.

I turn the key for the second door and push it open. Lo and behold, I'm inside! I'm in the room that has <u>mesmerized</u> me since I was a little girl. It is dark and dusty. I find a light switch and start my detective work.

There are lots of old boxes, the thick dark brown ones that you don't see anymore. There are also suitcases, the type that is rock hard and shaped like a box. Many suitcases these days are made of fabric and have wheels on them. How did they ever carry those heavy things? I wonder. It is just too dark because the only small window is covered by boxes and the light bulb just doesn't cast enough light. I run down and get my flashlight.

I'm back now, roaming around the room. Some bags are in the corner, covered by dust and spider webs. I open the closest box to me as I'm standing in the middle of the room. It was tightly <u>sealed</u> originally but the tape is dry now and not holding it together. I open slowly and see what's inside: old photo albums of pictures from the 1940s, a small box, with an <u>engraved</u> decoration on it, that smells of tobacco, and a strange pair of binoculars that I can see pictures in!

Wow! All this amazing stuff! Hang on . . . I see a corner of a treasure chest under those two boxes over on the left. I make my way there and pick up and push the boxes aside and get to the treasure chest.

Strangely enough, there isn't that much dust on it and hand prints on the dust look a bit fresh. I see a paper that doesn't look that old. It is taped to the chest with a message, "Sweetheart . . . we knew you would be here when we are away. Please don't open this. Wait for your 18th birthday, and we'll open this together. Now go back out of the attic and lock the door and do your homework!" (Signed, Mom and Dad).

COMPREHENSION

Answer the following questions. Use complete sentences.

1. Why do you think the writer was so curious about the attic?

   _____

2. What did Ty say was in the attic, to scare his sister?

   _____

3. Describe all the things the girl saw when she entered the attic.

   _____

4. What do you suppose the engraved box was used for?

   _____

5. How long does the girl have to wait until her parents let her see the contents of the treasure chest?

   _____

DISCUSSION

1. Is there an attic, or another secret place, in your house? Is there anything in this place?

2. Where did your parents hide things when you were younger? Was there a hiding place in your home?

3. At what age did you first stay home alone? Did you take good care of yourself? Did you do anything unusual?

4. How would you describe yourself as a teenager? What adjectives would you use?

Listening

◀)) *Track 2*

WHODUNNIT?

Detective Matheson is in charge of an investigation about a missing pet dog. He is interrogating the Yettie family. Listen to the audio.

COMPREHENSION

Answer the following questions. Use complete sentences.

1. Why is the detective already familiar with the Yettie family?

   _____

2. Why is the detective surprised that the family called him so early?

   _____

3. Who saw the dog last before it disappeared?

   _____

4. Why does the maid want extra pay?

   _____

5. Name the three negative qualities of the dog that the detective mentions at the end.

   _____

DISCUSSION

Fill in the chart on the following page. Which character do you think is guilty? Share your answers with your partner.

The characters mentioned in the audio are Mr. Yettie, Mrs. Yettie, Edward Yettie (the son), Ellie Yettie (the daughter), Marcus (the butler), Lila (the maid), and of course, Detective Matheson.

Name Of Character	Guilty? Why?
1.	yes / no / maybe
2.	yes / no / maybe
3.	yes / no / maybe
4.	yes / no / maybe
5.	yes / no / maybe
6.	yes / no / maybe

Writing

Do you own something that is valuable or important to you? What is it? Did you buy it yourself, or did someone give it to you? Write a short composition (about 200 words) about this item. Why is it special to you?

CHAPTER REVIEW

Summary

- Nouns can refer to people, places, or things. There are proper nouns and common nouns. Proper nouns are names of specific people or places and have a capital letter at the beginning. Common nouns begin with lower-case letters.

- Pronouns can replace nouns. Five common kinds are personal pronouns (which can serve as either subject or object in a sentence), possessive pronouns, reflexive pronouns, indefinite pronouns, and demonstrative pronouns.

EXERCISE 1

Fill in the blanks to correctly complete the sentences. Use each word from the list once.

milk	poverty	health	advice	luggage
oil	weather	glasses	rice	toothpaste

1. I don't really like pasta. I much prefer _____ with vegetables.

2. Good _____ is more important than lots of money.

3. I have a headache. I think I need new _____.

4. What is the best _____ for travelling around Europe—a backpack or a suitcase?

5. Many doctors recommend that you drink a glass of _____ every day.

6. I need to find a drugstore when we arrive in Calgary. I forgot to pack my _____.

7. Although I saw a lot of _____ in Africa, I loved the continent.

8. What is the _____ like in Iceland? Is it always very cold?

9. Are you frying peppers and mushrooms? Don't use too much _____.

10. We don't know how to invest our money. Maybe the bank will give us some _____.

EXERCISE 2

Fill in each blank with the correct plural form of the word in parentheses.

1. I would like to have three _____ (child).

2. We saw two _____ (mouse) under the tables in the restaurant.

3. It's autumn, so the _____ (leaf) are falling.

4. A group of _____ (woman) got on the bus.

5. She has cavities in two of her _____ (tooth).

EXERCISE 3

Fill in the blanks with *is* or *are*.

1. The team _____ playing well this season. Lakner and Watkins _____ especially good players.

2. My family _____ spending the winter in California. My grandparents _____ renting a house there.

3. The whole class _____ going to the museum. Dr. Talbot _____ giving a talk on dinosaurs.

4. Do you know when the committee _____ meeting to discuss the new budget?

5. There was a terrible tornado in Oklahoma. The army _____ helping people.

EXERCISE 4

Unscramble the following groups of words and make them into sentences. Add capital letters and punctuation where necessary.

1. fixed / himself / Guy / his motorcycle

_____

2. her hair / she / herself / cuts

_____

3. are mine / belong to / but these / those shoes / my sister

_____

4. is / mine / know / this bike / I

_____

5. gave / high fives / ourselves / we / after the game

_____

EXERCISE 5

Circle the letter of the correct pronoun to complete the sentences.

1. Those people listen to _____ iPods on the bus.
   a) his
   b) theirs
   c) their

2. Do you like our new bookshelves? We built them _____.
   a) themselves
   b) weselves
   c) ourselves

3. We always have dinner at home with _____ parents on Sundays.
   a) ours
   b) our
   c) them

4. _____ and I need to take the bus to school.
   a) We
   b) She
   c) Her

5. Those aren't your socks. They are _____.
   a) my
   b) hers
   c) your

EXERCISE 6

Fill in the blanks with the correct pronouns to complete the sentences.

1. Come here and help me with _____ zipper, please. _____ am late.

2. I don't really like _____ dress on the rack over there. I prefer _____ one here.

3. Wow! _____ cake is delicious! How did you make _____?

4. He hurt _____ skateboarding and had to call _____ father to come and take him home.

5. _____ sister's notebooks are on the table. I know they are _____ because they have _____ name on them.

EXERCISE 7

Fill in the blanks to correctly complete the sentences. Use each word from the list once.

anything	nothing	anyone	everybody	nobody

1. _____ wished her a happy birthday. She was very upset.

2. I'm hungry! Is there _____ to eat?

3. I left the party early because I didn't know _____ there.

4. The children are bored. They have _____ to do.

5. _____ screamed when the fire started.

Articles and Determiners

PART 1

1 SIMPLE PRESENT AND PRESENT PROGRESSIVE

2 NOUNS AND PRONOUNS

3 ARTICLES AND DETERMINERS

4 SIMPLE PAST, PAST PROGRESSIVE, *USED TO*

5 COMPARATIVES, SUPERLATIVES, AND EQUATIVES

6 THE FUTURE

OVERVIEW

- Articles *a*, *an*, and *the* come before a noun.
- Determiners also come before the nouns they modify. They indicate quantities of nouns.
- Determiners can be units of measurement; they tell us *how much* of the noun we have or need. We need to use the correct determiners with countable and non-countable nouns.

Warm-up

In pairs, take turns answering these questions.

- How often do you go shopping for food? What do you like to buy?
- What are some items that you prefer to buy in large amounts?
- What are some items that you prefer to buy in small amounts and more frequently?
- What are the four or five things that you absolutely must always have in your fridge at home?

ARTICLES

Articles can be either definite (*the*) or indefinite (*a* and *an*).

Warm-up

Work in pairs. Look at the pictures below. What do you think each picture is?

A: I think it's a man with an umbrella.

B: I think it's a giraffe.

A: That's the sky . . . and these are clouds.

Formation

- Place the article before the noun.
- We use the indefinite article *a* with a noun that we are talking about for the first time, or that is one of many:

    I have <u>a</u> cat and <u>a</u> dog.

    I'd like <u>a</u> glass of orange juice and <u>a</u> bagel, please.

- Before a vowel sound (a, e, i, o, u), *a* is changed to *an*:

  I had **an** egg for breakfast.　　　　He ordered **an** ice-cream sandwich.

  Ouch! There is **an** object in my eye.　　There's **an** umbrella in the car.

When the letter *u* is pronounced [yoo], we use *a*:

a university, **a** uniform

- The definite article *the* is used to refer to a specific noun—something that is known or that we have already talked about:

  I have **a** cat and **a** dog. **The** cat is white, and **the** dog is black.

  I'd like **a** glass of orange juice and **a** bagel, please. Can I have **the** bagel with butter and cheese?

- In English, when making a general statement about a plural noun, often no article is needed.

Singular Article	Plural Article	Example Sentences
the	the	This is **the** book I want to buy. That's **the** neighbour's cat. This is **the** book I was talking about. **The** neighbourhood children are playing outside.
a		**A** train can go very fast. **A** mobile phone shouldn't be the only means of communication. (general statement, mobile phone: singular)
an		**An** apple a day, keeps the doctor away.
Ø (no article)	Ø (no article)	Bicycles are very economical. Mobile phones are becoming more and more of a necessity in today's busy world. (general statement, mobile phones: plural)

EXERCISE 1

In the dialogue below, (circle) the correct article each time.

Angela is sick. The pharmacist told her to follow these instructions to get better.

Pharmacist:

Take (a / an / the / Ø) Aspirin every day. It doesn't matter what time of (a / an / the / Ø) day you take it. It is very important that you take the new Vitamin C pill that the doctor gave you every morning before breakfast. Don't forget, you should take (a / an / the / Ø) pill out of the bottle and you chew it. Do not swallow it. It is too big. (A / An / The) doctor has written (a / an / the / Ø) note that you should eat garlic for your high blood pressure. Just include it with your meals. You can take the stomach capsule after your lunch and after (a / an / the / Ø) snack. All this should help you feel better.

Now don't forget: "(A / An / The) apple a day keeps (a / an / the / Ø) doctor away."

Angela:

Thank you. You know what I always say, "(A / An / The) clove of garlic a day keeps everybody away!"

DETERMINERS

There are other categories of non-countable nouns. For example:

- **Natural Matter:** sand, air, soil, oxygen, water
- **Natural Phenomena:** lightning, magnetism, sunshine, weather, thirst, hunger
- **Ideas, Beliefs, Feelings:** selfishness, anger, kindness, generosity, capitalism, democracy
- **Subjects of Study:** history, chemistry, biology, geography, economics

Determiners are words that express the number or amount of the nouns mentioned. Which determiner is used depends on whether a noun is countable or non-countable.

In English, some nouns are considered countable and some non-countable.

Countable nouns have plural forms: oranges, doctors, schools, puppies, children.

Non-countable nouns do not have plural forms: equipment, luggage, jewellery, money, milk, furniture.

Groups of things that have countable parts are also non-countable.

- This is the room where we keep the soccer equipment.
(Equipment can include many items such as goal posts, nets, shin pads, uniforms, balls, scoreboard, etc.)

- We have some homework to do for English: an assignment and a presentation.
(Homework is non-countable, but an assignment can be plural: assignments.)

Warm-up

What do you look at while you are studying at home? Do you have a favourite poster on your wall? Choose from the list below, then share your ideas with a partner.

_____ a beautiful scene, like a beach or mountains

_____ a picture of a city, with lots of bright lights

_____ a simple picture, like a few flowers in a vase

_____ a picture of your favourite musical group or movie star

_____ something abstract, with many different colours and shapes

_____ a copy of a very well-known work of art

_____ something different?

Formation

USING THE CORRECT DETERMINERS

1 Determiners Used with Countable Nouns	Example Sentences
many	There are **many** apples in the basket. **Many** people were at the park for the fireworks.
several	**Several** books were overdue at the library. **Several** classes were cancelled on the day of the storm.
a few	We saw **a few** people at the bus stop. There are **a few** players still left on the field.
(very) few*	**Few** people were ready for the flood. The mayor was worried. I am new to this city. I know **very few** people.

2 Determiners Used with Non-countable Nouns	Example Sentences
much	Do you have **much** homework tonight?
a great deal (of)	The students spent **a great deal of** time on their homework that night.
a little	Please add **a little** salt to the spaghetti sauce.
(very) little*	Please hurry up; we have **very little** time.

*__Note__: _Few_ and _little_ without the article _a_ indicate a very small quantity or amount. The meaning is generally negative; in other words, you don't have as much or as many as you would like.

I have a few good friends. (positive) I have people I like and trust. I have very few good friends. (negative) I am lonely.

I have a little time. (positive) I can help you. I have very little time. (negative) I am feeling stressed.

3 Determiners Used with Both Countable and Non-countable Nouns	Example Sentences	
all (the)	**All** coffee is available to purchase by the bag.	**All** coins dropped at once onto the floor.
most	He spends **most** of his time in the library.	**Most** of his marks were passing grades.
a lot (of), lots (of)	**A lot of** sugar was used to make that iced tea. We need **lots of** money for our vacation.	**A lot of** people were hurt when the bridge collapsed. **Lots of** birds flocked over the water, calling loudly.
enough, plenty (of)	We have **enough** milk to make it through breakfast tomorrow. There is **plenty of** water to put out our campfire.	Do you have **enough** blankets to keep you warm? **Plenty of** books were available at 30 percent off during the sale.
some	**Some** nervousness is natural when you speak in front of an audience.	**Some** boats were sailing through the harbour on their way to the island.
none (of the), no	**None** of her friends was home when she called. **None** of the team was ready to go on the field.	**No** items were left on the shelves after the big sale. **No** team member was in the penalty box.

None of the players **is** on the field.   **Some** of the players **are** on the field.   **All** of the players **are** on the field.

EXERCISE 2

Paula and David are having dinner in a restaurant. Read their conversation with the server. On the next page, fill in each blank with a word in the list below. Use each word only once.

a little   the   no   some   a few   several   a lot of   an   a   Ø (nothing)

Server: Good evening. I'll be your server tonight. Let me tell you about our specials. We have _____ specials tonight. We have fish with _____ potatoes and vegetables, spaghetti Bolognese, and chicken curry.

David: Great. I'd like _____ fish, but can I have it with _____ vegetables and _____ potatoes? I'm on a diet. Oh, and I'd like a Caesar salad, but with only _____ salad dressing.

Server: And for you, ma'am?

Paula: May I have _____ omelette and fries? I only want _____ fries; I'm not very hungry.

Server: No problem. Can I get you some drinks?

Paula: I'll just have _____ glass of water, please. And can we have _____ bread?

David: Same for me, please.

Server: I'll be right back with your water.

EXERCISE 3

Circle the correct determiners in the following sentences. There may be more than one correct answer for each.

Our Lovely Planet

Our beautiful and lovely planet is going through (**a great deal of / many / some**) turmoil these days. In recent years we have had (**a lot of / much / many**) earthquakes followed by lots of dangerous tsunamis. Following (**plenty / few / many**) big quakes, there are also (**several / little / much**) aftershocks.

Many disastrous events are linked to the changes to the atmosphere. (**Much / Most**) people suspect that (**much / many / a little**) years of pollution have contributed to climatic changes. Last year alone, (**much / many / lots of**) floods caused a lot of the mudslides in parts of the west coast. Sometimes you see (**many / much / few**) of the forests burn because there isn't (**much / many / enough**) rain, while in the same country so many homes are flooded!

(**Much / Several / Little**) scientists and (**a few / some / most**) meteorologists have tried to force governments to make regulations to reduce pollution, but it is a slow process. There are (**most / few / enough**) skeptics left these days; almost (**all / much / no**) people agree that we have to take care of our lovely planet. If we (**none / some / all**) do a little every day to help, (**lots of / a lot of / a great deal of / several**) good change can happen.

EXERCISE 4

Artist Ken Kendall is talking about his life and work. Fill in each blank with an article or determiner (or leave it blank if nothing is needed). There may be more than one correct answer.

I'm _____ artist. I paint _____ abstract paintings. I painted 50 abstract paintings last year. I like to use _____ colours, but I do have _____ favourites: red, orange, and purple.

My career did not start well. I had a show at _____ big art gallery, but _____ of my paintings sold. I made _____ money. I lived in poverty for five years! Then, _____ famous art collector heard about me. She bought _____ of my paintings; _____ best one cost $2,000.

People ask me where I get my ideas from. I spend _____ time travelling. Last year, I spent _____ weeks in Australia. I want to travel more, but I don't have _____ time.

I work _____ days in the week. I paint _____ day, and I drink _____ cups of coffee while I work. In the evening, I sometimes go to _____ concert or _____ movie. I go to _____ bed early.

COMPARING AMOUNTS

Determiner	Comparative	Superlative
much / a lot of This company lost **much** information in the fire.	**more . . . than** This company lost **more** information in the fire **than** the company next door did.	**the most** This company lost **the most** information of all.
many / a lot of This company has **many** employees.	**more . . . than** That company has **more** employees **than** this one.	**the most** The company on the edge of town has **the most** employees of all.

Continued

Determiner	Comparative	Superlative
little / a little I have **little** free time.	**less . . . than** Jing has **less** free time **than** I do.	**the least** Kevin has **the least** free time of all of us.
a few We have **a few** pieces of furniture.	**fewer . . . than** Clair and Leo have **fewer** pieces of furniture **than** we do.	**the fewest** Carol and Trevor have **the fewest** pieces of furniture of all of us.

The correct spelling of the word we use to compare two things is *than*, NOT *then*.

You have less **than** 10 minutes to do the quiz.

EXERCISE 5

Fill in the blanks to correctly complete the sentences. Use a word or expression from the list. Some words may be used more than once.

| much | many | a lot of | more | the most | little | few | the least | the fewest |

1. Norbert has _____ CDs than Janet.

2. Jenny makes $12 per hour, Sue makes $13.50, and Petra makes $15. Petra makes _____ money of all the women.

3. Can you answer these emails? I have very _____ time and _____ other tasks to do.

4. Yasmine writes _____ poems. She wants to publish a book.

5. The Sutherlands have two grandchildren, the Chens have five, and the McGregors have eight. The Sutherlands have _____ grandchildren.

6. Emmanuel spends _____ of his time volunteering. He wins the prize for doing _____ volunteer work of all the students.

7. They live in a small town, so they have _____ opportunities to go to the theatre.

8. Isabella watches three hours of television per week, Mansour watches five hours, and Andreia watches twelve hours. Isabella watches _____ television of all of them.

EXPRESSING EQUALITY

Keywords	Use	Example Sentences
as many . . . as	To show that two groups of countable nouns are **equally large** in number	Alan has **as many pairs of shoes as** his brother does. Stella won **as many games of chess** as her sister did.
as few . . . as	To show that two groups of countable nouns are **equally small** in number	This lineup has **as few people as** the next one does. Belinda made **as few mistakes** on her grammar test as Roy did.
as much . . . as	To show that two amounts of non-countable nouns are **equally large** in number	She has **as much information** as I have. Chia drank **as much coffee** as Shu did.
as little . . . as	To show that two amounts of non-countable nouns are **equally small** in number	I can't help you. I have **as little money as** you have. They have **as little hope as** you have.

EXERCISE 6

Fill in the blanks to correctly complete the sentences. Use the words from the list. Look at the example to help you.

mistakes	software	~~information~~	advice	cookies
noise	research	cupcakes	talent	music

We wanted as much _____ as possible. → We wanted as much <u>information</u> as possible.

1. The children ate as many _____ as they could.

2. The company wanted to buy as much _____ as it could afford.

3. My mother ordered as many _____ from the caterer as the last time.

4. The director wanted as little _____ as possible during rehearsal.

5. I might win the singing contest. I have as much _____ as the other competitors!

6. You should try to make as few _____ as possible on the exam.

EXERCISE 7

Fill in the blanks. Use *much*, *many*, *few*, or *little*.

1. I didn't take as _____ vacation photos as my sister did.

2. I'll give you as _____ help as I can with your project.

3. Sandra's friends were very helpful; they gave her as _____ advice as her parents did.

4. Kyle drinks as _____ coffee as his wife; neither of them likes it.

5. We're moving to Florida, so we're trying to buy as _____ winter clothes as we can.

6. Hitomi didn't eat as _____ slices of pizza as Evan did.

COMMUNICATIVE ACTIVITY 1

With a partner, look at the information about the soccer teams listed in the box below. Discuss the teams' various wins and losses. In the space provided, write three positive sentences using *as . . . as*. Now exchange books with your partner and write three negative sentences using *not as . . . as* using your partner's sentences.

Team	Wins	Losses	Ties
Wildcats	6	4	2
Tigers	4	4	4
Bears	7	3	2
Hawks	6	3	3
Eagles	4	6	2
Lions	3	7	2

The Tigers have as many wins as losses.

The Eagles do not have as many losses as the Lions.

_____

_____

_____

_____

_____

_____

✥ COMMUNICATIVE ACTIVITY 2

Personal Habits

Walk around the room, asking your classmates questions about their activities and habits, and filling in their names and details in the appropriate space in the chart.

drinks coffee	exercises daily	studies English	likes walking	eats chocolate

Then write three sentences using *as . . . as* or *not as . . . as*.

> Nadia drinks two cups of coffee a day. Simon only drinks one cup of coffee in the morning. Simon does not drink as much coffee as Nadia.

_____

_____

_____

_____

_____

_____

BRINGING IT ALL TOGETHER

✥ COMMUNICATIVE ACTIVITY 3

Favourite Candy Bar Ingredients

Everyone brings in their favourite snack or candy bar to class. Work in groups of three or four.

Someone goes first and places the candy in the middle of the table. Everyone else in the group tries to guess the ingredients of the candy or snack bar. Use proper articles and determiners when listing ingredients.

After listening to everyone, the one who had brought in the candy bar reads the contents of the candy from the package. The one who guesses the best wins the candy.

There is lots of sugar, some nuts, and a little bit of butter and cocoa in this chocolate bar.

There is no caramel, but there is some honey and lots of raisins in this snack bar.

COMMUNICATIVE ACTIVITY 4

Name That Job!

What is important to you when choosing a job? Work in pairs. Look at the following descriptions, and choose the perfect job for each of these people.

1. "I like working with people. I like to meet lots of new people every day. I have plenty of energy. I take several trips each year, so I don't mind travelling."

   "You should be a/an _____."

2. "I am not a morning person! I do most of my work at night. I prefer to work alone, or with just a few other people. I don't like stressful environments. I have lots of creativity."

   "You should be a/an _____."

3. "I want to make a lot of money. I can work lots of hours in the week, and I only need a few short breaks every day. I don't need many vacations."

   "You should be a/an _____."

COMMUNICATIVE ACTIVITY 5

Your Choice!

Work in groups of four. Choose your answer to each of these questions, then discuss your answers with your group.

1. It's your birthday. Your friends are taking you out for a special dinner. You can eat anything you like. What do you choose?

   a) A burger, some fries, and a glass of cola
   b) A spicy dish, like curry and rice
   c) Lots of salad and fresh fruit

   d) Other _____

2. Hooray! All of your classes are cancelled today. What do you plan to do?

   a) Call a friend, see a movie, and perhaps go to the mall.
   b) Do lots of homework; you want to get ahead in your courses.
   c) Go to the gym, play a sport, or take an exercise class.

   d) Other _____

3. You see a friend cheating on a test. What do you do?

    a) Tell the teacher; cheating is wrong.
    b) Nothing—friendship is more important.
    c) Ignore it. All students cheat sometimes.

    d) Other _____

4. You win $10,000 in the lottery. What do you do with the money?

    a) Put it in the bank.
    b) Buy a new computer, or some new clothes.
    c) Take a trip with a few close friends.

    d) Other _____

Reading

Read the passage and answer the questions that follow.

KIAN'S PICTURES

Kian is a 75-year-old man living at a <u>retirement</u> home in Georgetown, Barbados. Kian was born in Halifax, Canada, but lived most of his life in Boston, Massachusetts, USA. These days Kian is in good hands at the retirement home where they take good care of him. He is, after all, a celebrity.

Kian is the famous painter of dream houses. No one can believe that he has never had a house of his own, yet he painted some of the most beautiful houses people can only dream about.

Kian grew up an <u>orphan</u> and lived in different foster homes until he moved to Montreal as a young man and studied fine arts. With so many years as a student and a young man trying to make ends meet, he never had much money. He didn't have a chance to save enough money for a house of his own.

He made most of his living by painting pictures of houses. When he was 25, a <u>real-estate agent</u> named Ramin Singh bought one of his paintings to display at his office. Soon Ramin noticed that people who came in to see him about purchasing a home often commented on the painting and even said, "We want to <u>purchase</u> a house like the one in that picture."

Ramin went looking to find Kian and after finding him quite poor, offered him a good salary to paint more images of dream homes. About a couple of years later, many real-estate agents' and <u>architects'</u> offices and personal homes were displaying Kian's paintings. By this time, three original homes had been built that were inspired by his paintings and lots more were built in the years to come. Outside one of these homes is a plaque that reads, "The design of this home was inspired by Kian, the painter."

Kian's paintings had details and colours that left viewers in awe. In one particular painting, he shows the details of the roof, the lights and shadows and even the shadow of a bird flying over the roof. Below, he shows each and every brick of the front of the house, and the one middle corner brick that has <u>eroded</u> and discoloured. This is how he made all his paintings look real.

His paintings are of the imagination, a world where homes are delightful to look at and to live in; however, Kian himself never got to live in any home that looked like his own pictures. He travelled to promote his paintings while fighting health problems with his lungs. He paid an enormous amount of money to <u>maintain</u> his health and is still struggling with it.

He is finally settled down on this beautiful island today, but he may only have a little time left. He needs the medical care of retirement living with a nurse checking on him frequently.

Although Kian never fulfilled his own dream of owning and living in a beautiful house with a view of the river, a grand entrance, a bay window, or any of those luxurious extras of a <u>mansion</u>, he did <u>inspire</u> many builders, designers, and architects. Today his art is famous for inspiration and his fans visit him at the retirement home and show him pictures of their own homes, which were inspired by his paintings.

COMPREHENSION

Answer the following questions. Use complete sentences.

1. Did Kian have much money or success as a young man? Explain.

   _____

2. In which offices did Kian's paintings first appear?

   _____

3. Give some examples of the kinds of details found in Kian's paintings.

   _____

4. What is the main reason why he can't live in a house today?

   _____

5. Which professional people get their ideas from Kian's work?

   _____

Listening

 *Track 3*

LOST AND FOUND

Listen to the audio. You will hear a dialogue between a tourist and a museum attendant at the Metropolitan Museum of Art.

COMPREHENSION

Listen again and complete the following chart.

Article	Item	Quantity	At the Lost and Found?
	Japanese passport		
	German passports	two	✓
a	gold pen	one	✗
	gold key ring		
	athletic shoes		
	navy folding binder		
	map of New York		
	amusement park map		
	bus schedule		
	brochure		
	backpack		
	pens		
	camera		
	navy leather wallet		
	writing pads		
	Met picture books		
	Kumiko's friends		
	ink pen		
	iPad		

DISCUSSION

Work in pairs. Discuss the following questions with your partner.

1. Which items do people lose most often in museums?

2. Where was Kumiko when she noticed her passport was missing?

3. How many passports does Albert have?

4. Why are these passports not Kumiko's?

5. What does Kumiko keep inside her folding binder? Name three items.

6. What is the third item Kumiko has lost?

In your opinion, what is the worst thing to lose in a large building like a museum? (It could be, for example, your wallet, your passport, the name of your hotel, your travel companions.) Explain why.

Writing

Write a short composition (about 200 words) describing your favourite room in your home.

Describe everything that is in this room in detail and then explain why you like it so much. Where possible, use words like *a/an*, *the*, *some*, *several*, *many*, *enough*, *few*, and so on.

CHAPTER REVIEW

Summary

- Articles are either definite or indefinite. The definite article *the* is used for specific nouns, singular or plural. The indefinite article *a* or *an* is used for singular nouns or in general statements.

- Determiners are words that give information about the quantity of the noun: how much or how many. Countable nouns use determiners such as *many*, and non-countable nouns use determiners such as *much*. Some determiners, such as *a lot of* or *lots of*, can go with both countable and non-countable nouns.

EXERCISE 1

Circle the most appropriate article in parentheses. Choose Ø for no article.

1. This is (a / an / the / Ø) same girl I was telling you about yesterday.

2. (A / An / The / Ø) apple a day keeps (a / an / the / Ø) doctor away.

3. (A / An / The / Ø) Caribbean Islands have (a / an / the / Ø) warm climate.

4. (A / An / The / Ø) people should be respectful to the elderly.

5. I don't have (a / an / the / Ø) clue what you're talking about.

6. We stayed in (a / an / the / Ø) good hotel on our vacation.

7. Jim is in (a / an / the / Ø) bathroom. He's taking (a / an / the / Ø) shower.

8. I want to go to (a / an / the / Ø) new Italian restaurant and order (a / an / the / Ø) pizza.

9. There was (a / an / the / Ø) great movie on TV last night.

10. Stefanie wants to be (a / an / the / Ø) actor when she grows up.

EXERCISE 2

There are six determiner errors in the following paragraph. Find and correct them.

Years ago, when calculators first became popular among students, much math teachers were concerned that perhaps any young people would forget their times tables and rely on their calculators. Today, a little language teachers are concerned that students won't develop handwriting skills because they spend many of their time typing on a keyboard. You just have to walk into a college or university classroom and you see almost all of the students have a laptop or an iPad and take notes electronically. Many of their assignments are typed and they also type when they do their research online. There have been a lots of changes in the classrooms in the last a few decades. I wonder how many more changes are yet to come.

EXERCISE 3

Fill in each blank with *much*, *many*, *a lot of*, *more . . . than*, or *the most*.

1. Elena spent _____ time planning her trip to London.

2. She read _____ guidebooks and found _____ information online.

3. However, she got _____ advice from her English friends than from the library or the Internet.

4. For example, she learned that London hotels cost _____ money than hotels in Toronto or Ottawa.

5. She also discovered that she could see _____ famous sites in one day if she planned her time well.

6. She decided to visit some shops and parks, but to spend _____ time in the world-famous museums.

7. They don't cost _____ money; in fact, _____ of them are free!

8. Elena is hoping to have _____ fun in London.

Simple Past, Past Progressive, *Used to*

PART 1

1 SIMPLE PRESENT AND PRESENT PROGRESSIVE

2 NOUNS AND PRONOUNS

3 ARTICLES AND DETERMINERS

4 SIMPLE PAST, PAST PROGRESSIVE, *USED TO*

5 COMPARATIVES, SUPERLATIVES, AND EQUATIVES

6 THE FUTURE

OVERVIEW

- We use the simple past to talk about an action that happened in the past and that is now finished.

- To indicate a continuous action in the past, we use the past progressive.

- We use *used to* to describe an action or situation that happened in the past on a regular basis, but that we no longer do.

SIMPLE PAST

Warm-up

Work in small groups. Take turns talking about your vacation; use the pictures to guide you.

Student A:
You went to Cuba for your vacation. Tell your partners everything you did on your vacation.

Student B:
You went to Mont Tremblant, Quebec, for your vacation. Tell your partners everything you did on your vacation.

Formation

REGULAR VERBS

Positive Statement	Negative Statement	Yes / No Question	Wh- (Information) Question
I (you, he, she, it, we, you, they) **danced**.	I (you, he, she, it, we, you, they) **didn't dance**.	**Did** I (you, he, she, it, we, you, they) **dance**?	**Where** did I (you, he, she, it, we, you, they) **dance**?

The chart above shows how to form regular past tense verbs. Irregular verbs have a different construction; these are shown in Appendix A. Some common irregular past tense examples are shown on the following page.

IRREGULAR VERBS: *BE*, *HAVE*, AND *DO*

Positive Statement	Negative Statement	Yes / No Question	Wh- (Information) Question
I **was** there. You **were** there. He / She / It **was** there. We **were** there. You **were** there. They **were** there.	I **was not (wasn't)** there. You **were not (weren't)** there. He / She / It **was not (wasn't)** there. We **were not (weren't)** there. You **were not (weren't)** there. They **were not (weren't)** there.	**Was** I there? **Were** you there? **Was** he / she / it there? **Were** we there? **Were** you there? **Were** they there?	Where **was** I? Where **were** you? Where **was** he / she / it? Where **were** we? Where **were** you? Where **were** they?
I (you, he, she, it, we, you, they) **had** it.	I (you, he, she, it, we, you, they) **didn't have** it.	**Did** I (you, he, she, it, we, you, they) **have** it?	Why **did** I (you, he, she, it, we, you, they) **have** it?
I (you, he, she, it, we, you, they) **did** it.	I (you, he, she, it, we, you, they) **didn't do** it.	**Did** I (you, he, she, it, we, you, they) **do** it?	How **did** I (you, he, she, it, we, you, they) **do** it?

EXERCISE 1

Using Appendix A, complete the chart with the simple past tense of the verbs listed in the first column. Both regular and irregular verbs are included. Use each past tense verb in a sentence.

	Present	Past	Example Sentence
1	sing	sang	The choir sang beautifully.
2	lay		
3	travel		
4	sleep		
5	feel		
6	fall		
7	fail		
8	keep		

EXERCISE 2

Change each of the following positive sentences into the negative.

1. They travelled all over the world.

_____

2. She liked her new car.

   _____

3. The bus stopped outside the library.

   _____

4. It rained during the night.

   _____

5. Diana bought a new leather jacket.

   _____

6. Peter sold his bicycle to his friend.

   _____

EXERCISE 3

Change each of the following sentences into a yes / no question.

1. We were late.

   _____?

2. Felix climbed the tree to see the view.

   _____?

3. She received an unusual gift.

   _____?

4. They stayed in Florida all winter.

   _____?

5. His uncle drove his car for a week.

   _____?

6. Darlene's mother knew the password.

   _____?

EXERCISE 4

Change each of the following sentences to a wh- (information) question. The information you want to ask about is **bolded** and <u>underlined.</u>

1. Tristan played basketball with **his friends**.

   _____?

2. Linh called her father **every week**.

   _____?

3. Juan wanted a glass of water **because he was so thirsty**.

   _____?

4. They **developed an amazing project** for the company.

   _____?

5. The ride to Vancouver took **four hours**.

   _____?

6. The marathon was **42.2 kilometres** long.

   _____?

⚙ COMMUNICATIVE ACTIVITY 1

Back in the Day

Work in small groups. Each person takes a piece of paper, and writes the name of a toy he or she had as a child. Mix the papers and put them in the middle of the table. One by one, each group member picks a paper and asks the following questions:

- Whose paper is this?
- Why did you choose this toy?
- How did you play with it?
- Who did you play with?

You can add any other questions about the toy. Be sure to use the past tense.

⚙ COMMUNICATIVE ACTIVITY 2

Truth or Bluff?

Work in pairs.

Partner A: Think of a story to tell your partner. This could be a true story about something strange that happened to you, or it could be a made-up story. Think of as many details as you can. Tell the story to your partner.

Partner B: You need to guess whether the story is true or not. Ask your partner questions about the details in the story. Then, guess whether your partner is telling the truth or bluffing.

PAST PROGRESSIVE

Warm-up

On a piece of paper, write the following sentence and complete it:

At seven o'clock yesterday evening, I was _____ing _____.

At seven o'clock yesterday evening, I was taking my dog for a walk.

At seven o'clock yesterday evening, I was eating an apple.

Now write this sentence:

At seven o'clock yesterday evening, _____ was also _____-ing _____.

Move around the classroom. Ask your classmates, "What were you doing at seven o'clock yesterday evening?" Try to find someone who was doing the same as you. Tell the class who you found.

Formation

Positive Statement	Negative Statement	Yes / No Question	Wh- (Information) Question
I **was** singing. You **were** singing. He / She / It **was** singing. We **were** singing. You **were** singing. They **were** singing.	I **wasn't** singing. You **weren't** singing. He / She / It **wasn't** singing. We **weren't** singing. You **weren't** singing. They **weren't** singing.	**Was** I singing? **Were** you singing? **Was** he / she / it singing? **Were** we singing? **Were** you singing? **Were** they singing?	Where **was** I singing? Where **were** you singing? Where **was** he / she / it singing? Where **were** we singing? Where **were** you singing? Where **were** they singing?

The past progressive is formed by using the simple past form of the verb *be* and the root of the main verb plus *-ing*.

drive → I was driving, we were driving

run → I was running, we were running

USE

Use the past progressive for an action that started before a specific time and continued after it:

At eight o'clock yesterday evening, I was washing my hair.

When I woke up at six o'clock, the sun was already shining.

In some cases, we use the past progressive to show that two continuing actions were happening at the same time:

I was talking to Adele while I was driving.

Andy was cleaning the windows while Susan was polishing the furniture.

When one completed action follows another, use the simple past for both:

I got up, got dressed, and drove to school.

I turned the light off before I fell asleep.

When a shorter action interrupts a longer action, use the past progressive for the longer action:

Jenny slipped on the ice while she was walking home.

Kevin broke his ankle while he was playing hockey.

Note that the word *while* often indicates the past progressive tense.
The action in the past progressive may end, or it may continue:

While the plane was taking off, its engines failed and it crashed.

While we were walking home, it started to rain.

As with the present progressive, there are some verbs that we don't use in the past progressive. See the section Stative Verbs in Chapter 1 on page 11 for a list of these non-progressive verbs.

EXERCISE 5

Fill in each blank with the past progressive form of the verb in parentheses.

1. My aunt _____ (cook) while I _____ (wash) the dishes.

2. The bus driver _____ (drive) while we _____ (watch) the scenery.

3. The mother _____ (feed) her baby while her other children _____ (play) in the back yard.

4. The cars _____ (wait) at the red light while the ambulance _____ (try) to pass through.

5. The turtles _____ (walk) slowly while the rabbits _____ (run) through the hills.

EXERCISE 6

Change each of the following positive sentences into the negative.

1. Shiva was sharing lots of interesting ideas. (Use *any*.)

_____

2. They were stopping at every red light.

_____

3. We were barbecuing hot dogs and burgers.

_____

4. The students were writing the final exam.

_____

5. The teacher was marking the assignments.

_____

EXERCISE 7

Maggi can't find her laptop and she thinks her classmate, Sylvie, stole it. Maggi last saw her laptop at eight o'clock last night in the college library. She went to find a book, and her laptop disappeared. The college security team is investigating.

Read the conversation between the security guard and Sylvie. (Circle) the correct verb form to complete the sentences.

Security guard: Something (happened / was happening) last night in the library.

Someone (stole / was stealing) Maggi's laptop. What (did you do / were you doing) at eight o'clock last night?

Sylvie: I (watched / was watching) a movie. I (went / was going) to the movie theatre. I (didn't go / wasn't going) anywhere near the library all day.

Security guard: Who were you with?

Sylvie: I was alone. My boyfriend (wanted / was wanting) to come with me, but right after I (arrived / was arriving) at the theatre, he (sent / was sending) me a text. He (studied / was studying) for a test, and he couldn't come.

Security guard: (Did you see / Were you seeing) anyone?

Sylvie: While I (waited / was waiting) for the movie to start, I (saw / was seeing) my friend Laura, but she (didn't notice / wasn't noticing) me.

Security guard: So you have no proof that you were at the movies?

Sylvie: I guess not—but while I (sat / was sitting) in the theatre, I suddenly (felt / was feeling) hungry. I (bought / was buying) an ice cream. Someone might remember me.

Security guard: (Did anything strange happen / Was anything strange happening) in the middle of the movie?

Sylvie: No-o-o . . . why?

Security guard: I (called / was calling) the movie theatre. In the middle of the movie, while everyone (watched / was watching) the screen, the fire alarm (rang / was ringing). Everyone (left / was leaving) the theatre. They (didn't come / weren't coming) back.

Sylvie: Oh . . . um . . .

Security guard: Sylvie, what time (did you arrive / were you arriving) at the library last night?

EXERCISE 8

The security guard interviewed several other people about Maggi's stolen laptop. Read the answers below, and write the correct question.

1. Emily, where _____ at eight o'clock?

    I was in the sports centre.

2. Trevor, who _____ at eight o'clock?

    I was eating dinner with my parents.

3. What _____ at eight o'clock?

    Will and Martin were in the cafeteria, talking about tonight's hockey game.

4. Why _____ at eight o'clock?

    Valeria was carrying a large bag because she wanted to check some books out of the library.

5. Brad and Ellen, when _____?

    We were studying in the library from 8:30 until 10:00 PM.

6. Tom, what _____?

    While my girlfriend was looking for a book, I was surfing the Internet.

❖ COMMUNICATIVE ACTIVITY 3

Your Day in Court

Read the following situation:

> Gemma's Jewellery Store had a break-in recently. Someone stole a diamond and sapphire ring from the store at around midnight. The famous jewellery thief Sam Sparkle is on trial for the crime.

Work in groups of six or seven. You are going to act out a court scene. Decide who will play each of the following characters:

- Sam Sparkle
- the defence lawyer
- the prosecutor
- the judge
- witnesses

Using the information on the card your teacher gives you, ask and answer questions about the night of the crime. At the end, the judge should decide whether or not Sam is guilty.

USED TO

Warm-up

Work in groups of three. Complete the sentences below using names of people from your home country. Tell your classmates about these people.

_____ used to be a famous entertainer when I was a child.

_____ used to play professional sports, but he / she is now retired.

_____ used to be a great political leader many years ago.

_____ used to be liked and respected, but he / she is now unpopular.

Formation

- We use *used to . . .* when we're talking about something we did often, or regularly, in the past, but which we no longer do.
- The action must be something that happened many times or that continued for a long period of time.
- *Used to . . .* is followed by the base form of the verb.

  I used to ride my bicycle everywhere; now, I drive a car.

  I used to live in Toronto; now, I live in Montreal.

  I used to be a vegetarian; now, I eat meat.

What do you notice happens in the negative sentences and the questions?

Positive Statement	Negative Statement	Yes / No Question	Wh- (Information) Question
I used to **swim.**	I **didn't** use to **swim.**	**Did** I use to **swim?**	Where **did** you use to **swim?**
You used to **swim.**	You **didn't** use to **swim.**	**Did** you use to **swim?**	Where **did** you use to **swim?**
He / She / It used to **swim.**	He / She / It **didn't** use to **swim.**	**Did** he / she / it use to **swim?**	Where **did** he / she / it use to **swim?**
We used to **swim.**	We **didn't** use to **swim.**	**Did** we use to **swim?**	Where **did** we use to **swim?**
You used to **swim.**	You **didn't** use to **swim.**	**Did** you use to **swim?**	Where **did** you use to **swim?**
They used to **swim.**	They **didn't** use to **swim.**	**Did** they use to **swim?**	Where **did** they use to **swim?**

Used to changes slightly after the auxiliary *did*: it loses the *d*: *did + use to.*

Do not confuse *used to* with the expression *to be used to*.

Use *I am used to* when talking about something you do or experience regularly now, and that you are very comfortable doing.

I grew up in northern Canada. I am used to cold weather.

I am used to getting up early, so morning classes are no problem for me.

Henry felt ill because he wasn't used to eating spicy food.

To be used to is followed by a noun, or by the *-ing* form of the verb.

EXERCISE 9

Work in pairs. Read each sentence below, and then change it to a sentence using *used to* or *use to*.

Olga competed in dance auditions. → Olga used to compete in dance auditions.

1. We took the train.

2. Jessica sang in the shower.

3. Mirna cooked on weekends.

4. I didn't like cheese, but now I think it's okay.

5. Edmund didn't have long hair.

6. This restaurant didn't serve healthy food.

7. Did you ride horses as a child?

8. Did Rose smoke when she was young?

EXERCISE 10

Circle the correct verb form to complete the sentences.

1. Kelsey (**used to / was used to**) have blonde hair; now she is a brunette.

2. Tom grew up on a farm, so he (**used to / is used to**) waking up early.

3. I feel seasick! I (**didn't use to / am not used to**) sailing.

4. (**Did you use to / Are you used to**) drink milk as a child?

5. People in the past (**used to / were used to**) walk to school; today, children (**used to / are used to**) taking the school bus every day.

✦ COMMUNICATIVE ACTIVITY 4

Not Anymore

Work in small groups. Your teacher will give you some cards. Take turns asking each other the questions on the cards. When someone asks you a question, try to give as much information as you can.

BRINGING IT ALL TOGETHER

✦ COMMUNICATIVE ACTIVITY 5

Good and Bad Habits

good   bad   indifferent

Form groups of three or four. Your teacher will give you some cards with good and bad habits shown on them.

Student A: Choose one of these habits and make a sentence using *used to*.

Students B and C: Decide whether you think that action was a good habit, a bad habit, or a habit that you have no strong feelings about (are indifferent to). Student A can try to persuade you to change your decision.

Change roles and continue with the other habits.

Here's an example:

eating too much chocolate

"I used to eat too much chocolate." → "That's a bad habit."

"But I ate dark chocolate." → "Then I'm indifferent."

Reading

Read the passage and answer the questions that follow.

Last month, my wife asked me to clean the garage. She used to ask me to clean it every weekend, but that is when I like to chill out—you know, rest and relax.

Finally last weekend I got the nerve to get up and tidy up. After I discarded a whole bunch of old papers and boxes of junk, I came across a plastic storage box labelled "Bicycle Diaries of Don and Luc."

I looked at the box and stared at it for maybe 15 minutes. Then I finally opened it and had a pleasant surprise. You see, I had kept all the details of my youthful travels in this box. At that moment, I was looking into my past as if it was on a movie screen. Everything was coming to me in a flash, like a movie trailer.

In this box was everything to jog my memory. You see, when I finished high school, I was 19 and my buddy Luc was 18. We used to get together and talk about the places we wanted to visit, and the things we wanted to do. We decided to backpack across Europe. In this box are all the pictures of all the places we visited and all the people we met. There was the old T-shirt with "I love London" across the front and a mug with "J'aime Paris," brochures and maps—and, yes, a bicycle seat!

You are probably wondering, "What was a bicycle seat doing in the box?" Well, there are many stories from our European adventure, but the bicycle tops all of them.

You see, one day, when we were crossing the Channel from England to France, we met some amazing fellow backpackers from Spain and Portugal on the bus. They were so enthusiastic about cycling that they were on their way to watch the famous bicycle race, the Tour de France.

The entire ride, they told us all the details of the sport and who was their favourite, and who was winning. By the time we arrived, we had become interested in the sport ourselves.

Now, usually, when people tell travel stories, they tell about losing passports or misplacing luggage. Rarely do you ever hear of gaining items—particularly brand new bicycles!

As luck would have it, when all the passengers got off the bus, my buddy Luc was looking for his cellphone and so we were the last to get off. When we got off, the driver was standing by the luggage compartment and shouting, "Hurry up and take your boxes; I'm on a schedule!"

We replied, "We don't have boxes, just these backpacks." He said angrily, "I don't have time for games. You came with these giant boxes, you leave with them!"

"But . . ."

"No buts! It took me half an hour to fit them here with all the passengers waiting. Now you don't want them! I will have security come and escort you out of the station! Guard!"

Nothing we said or did worked. We looked at the boxes, looked at each other and after a brief moment, <u>shrugged our shoulders</u>. We realized we had no choice, so we carried those heavy trapezoid-shaped boxes to the front desk of the station in Paris and left them there. They took our names and the name of the <u>hostel</u> we were staying at. We didn't think much of it and walked to our hostel.

Two days later there was a message at the hostel that we were to be at the station to pick up something. We were confused, but we were curious enough to go and find out.

It turned out the boxes were never claimed and the wet washed-off address labels were now <u>illegible</u>. So, as unbelievable as it may seem, we were the new owners of the two boxes.

What was in them? Brand new racing bicycles!

This is only the beginning of the story. There is so much to tell: how we cycled all over France and Italy, how we were mistaken for <u>professional</u> cyclists, how we were offered free accommodation and meals, how we got into accidents twice and had one of the bikes stolen, how we lost each other in Austria and found one another through bicycle shops, how all that was left of our amazing gift was one bicycle seat, how we laughed for years over it, and how my buddy Luc lost a bet and I ended up keeping the seat . . .

I used to be so young and carefree, but that was a long time ago. The last time I spoke with Luc was three Christmases ago. I don't know what he's up to these days.

Yesterday I picked up the phone and called his brother and got his address. I told him I was sending Luc a surprise parcel. I was so excited that I couldn't wait, so I sent an express package with one-day delivery.

An hour ago, Luc sent me a text:

"Hahaha! I have been laughing since the doorbell rang and the delivery guy gave me a box with a bicycle seat in it!"

I called him and we laughed some more. We're meeting next weekend for some serious catch-up time and <u>reminiscing</u> about the good old days.

COMPREHENSION

Answer the following questions. Use complete sentences.

1. Where did Don find the box?

   _____

2. Why did he not want to open the box immediately?

   _____

3. What did Don and Luc use to do at ages 18 and 19?

   _____

4. Name some of the things Don found in the box.

   _____

5. Where were Don and Luc when they got the two bicycles?

   _____

6. Why did Don and Luc take the bicycles to the front desk of the station?

   _____

7. How did they manage to keep the bicycles?

   _____

8. Describe their travels around Europe with the bicycles.

   _____

9. How is Don and Luc's friendship different today?

   _____

10. What did Don do with the bicycle seat at the end?

   _____

DISCUSSION

1. Do you have a close friendship like the one Don and Luc had? Tell the class about your friend.

2. What was your best travel experience?

3. Don says, "I used to be so young and carefree, but that was a long time ago." Has your personality also changed? In what way(s) are you different from how you used to be?

Listening

◀)) *Track 4*

TRAVEL TALES

Listen to the audio.

COMPREHENSION

Fill in the blanks in the chart on the next page, using the correct words from the audio.

Conversation 1: At Vancouver International Airport

Vancouver International Airport	Would all passengers who _____ a ticket on Flight AC 458 to Punta Cana, Dominican Republic, please _____ now at the boarding gate.

	Roberta Steinbeck	Jimmy	Man
Questions Asked	Where _____ the _____ desk?	_____ you _____ that?	Did you _____ information desk?
Responses		I _____ know.	Yes, I _____.
Comments	It _____ very clear, but you _____ my name.		They _____ them at half price too!

Conversation 2: At the Ottawa Train Station

	Mark	Laila
Comments	When we first met, you _____ me how much you always _____ to see Niagara Falls.	My family _____ to Europe or North Africa for holidays.
Questions Asked	_____ you like the wedding cake _____?	Did _____ think it _____ too much _____?
Responses	I _____ notice the sugar.	I _____ it very sweet.
Comments	I _____ everyone liked it.	

Ottawa Train Station	Train 112 to Niagara Falls is now _____. Passengers are to _____ one hour and twenty minutes or go to Counter 45 to _____ travel tickets.

DISCUSSION

Work in pairs. Answer the following questions in complete sentences.

At Vancouver International Airport

1. Who first realized that the message was for Roberta?

   _____

2. Where did Roberta need to go?

   _____

3. Do you think the man gave good directions? Why, or why not?

   _____

4. What used to be in the airport that isn't there now: (a) an elevator; (b) a coffee shop; or (c) a shoe store?

   _____

At the Ottawa Train Station

1. Where were Mark and Laila going?

   _____

2. What event were they celebrating?

   _____

3. How long was the train delayed?

   _____

4. How did Mark and Laila react to the delay?

   _____

5. Did Mark and Laila decide to wait, or did they exchange their tickets?

   _____

6. Why do you think they waited a long time to get married?

   _____

Writing

Describe the life of someone you used to know who was generous and did good deeds. Write a short composition (150 to 200 words) to describe this person's past actions. If there isn't anyone you knew personally, use a famous good-hearted person like Mother Teresa.

CHAPTER REVIEW

Summary

Use	Form	Keywords	Positive Statement	Negative Statement	Yes / No Question
completed action in the past	**Simple Past** Regular verbs: root form of verb + -ed Irregular verbs: refer to Appendix A	yesterday, a week ago, last year, 10 years ago, last Saturday, two days ago, all day long, in 1996	He played in his neighbourhood last week.	He didn't play in his neighbourhood last week.	Did he play in his neighbourhood last week?
continued action in the past	**Past Progressive** was / were + root form of verb + -ing	while, as	While he was waiting at the subway station, he was reading his book. As he was approaching the top of the mountain, it started to snow.	He wasn't waiting at the subway station. He wasn't reading his book.	Was he waiting at the subway station?
action in the past that was done habitually but is probably discontinued now	used to + infinitive	used to / did not (didn't) use to	He used to play sports but he doesn't anymore because of his injuries.	He didn't use to play sports.	Did he use to play sports?

EXERCISE 1

Change the simple present to the simple past in the following paragraphs. Pay attention to spelling and correct forms of the verbs.

The weather is so cold. There is a lot of wind. It blows at 80 kilometres an hour!

It nearly knocks down the old tree by the side of the road. It is scary to watch. We see everything move right and left. It is unbelievable. I think it is a good idea to take cover and protect ourselves. We go to the basement where we are safer.

The electricity is off! We don't have light, we don't have radio, and we don't have an Internet connection either.

Why don't we sit by the fireplace and drink some tea? Because our electric kettle doesn't work without electricity! Oh, what an experience this is!

EXERCISE 2

Change the present progressive to the past progressive in the following paragraphs. Pay attention to spelling and correct forms of the verbs; you might need to change some simple present tense verbs to the simple past.

We are sitting in the cafeteria and our friend Joe is coming over to talk to us. We love Joe's stories. He is always telling the most interesting stories. He is always travelling somewhere new and coming back and sharing his stories with us.

He is telling us such an interesting story that we don't want to leave the table and go to class. We are sitting in the cafeteria and we are looking at the clock and our watches and we are still sitting after an hour. We are going to be late for class.

You see, he is telling the story of how he drove by the coastline and crossed the border and didn't notice it. We are sitting on the edge of our seats, holding our breath, wondering what we are doing in the cafeteria when our professor is speaking in the lecture hall already. We are wondering now how Joe returned and what happened next when all of a sudden someone is shouting, "Test today in class!"

We are running faster than you can imagine! Next time in the cafeteria we are telling our story!

EXERCISE 3

Fill in the blanks to correctly complete the sentences. Use *used to . . .*, *didn't use to. . .*, or *did you use to . . .*

Amy: Mom, tell me about when you were a little girl. Where _____

        live?

Mom: We _____ have a house on Oak Street, not far from here. We had a big garden, with a treehouse. Uncle Nick and I _____ play in the treehouse almost every day.

Amy: _____ get along?

Mom: Most of the time. We were lucky; we _____ fight very often. He was a pretty good big brother.

Amy: What else _____ do?

Mom: I _____ walk to school. I _____ like reading or writing, but now I enjoy it. I _____ enjoy doing chores at home, either, but I had no choice. I _____ help Grandma with the cooking and the ironing.

Amy: What _____ want to be when you grew up?

Mom: I _____ want to be a flight attendant, but now I'm glad I became a full-time mom.

Amy: Me too!

Comparatives, Superlatives, and Equatives

PART 1

1 SIMPLE PRESENT AND PRESENT PROGRESSIVE

2 NOUNS AND PRONOUNS

3 ARTICLES AND DETERMINERS

4 SIMPLE PAST, PAST PROGRESSIVE, *USED TO*

5 COMPARATIVES, SUPERLATIVES, AND EQUATIVES

6 THE FUTURE

OVERVIEW

- There are three basic ways to compare people, places, or things. If differences are expressed, then we use comparative or superlative forms, depending on how many items are being compared.

- The comparative form is used to compare two people, places, or things and uses the word *than*.

  Hockey is more popular than soccer in Canada.

  Arshad swims more gracefully than Arlene.

- The superlative form is used to compare one person or thing with the rest of the group it belongs to and uses the definite article *the*.

  Soccer is the most popular sport in the world.

  Arshad swims the most gracefully of anyone on the team.

- The equative form is used to show that two people, places, or things are the same in some way and uses *as . . . as*.

  Soccer is as fun as hockey.

  Arlene swims as quickly as Arshad.

COMPARATIVE AND SUPERLATIVE ADJECTIVES

Warm-up

sports car

minivan

luxury car

basic car

Look at the cars in the pictures. Make sentences to compare them. Use as many adjectives as you can think of.

> The sports car is faster than the minivan.

Which car would you like to own? Why?

> Nouns may act like adjectives in certain instances:
>
> The team has five members. (*Members* is a noun.) That is a five-member team. (*Five* + *member* combine to form a "compound adjective.")

Formation

- Adjectives give information about nouns and they generally appear before the nouns that they modify.
- Adjectives are never plural, even if the nouns that they modify are.

  > The top-scoring hockey players from each team won a free vacation.

- The formation of the comparative and superlative forms of adjectives depends on the spelling of the adjective.

COMPARATIVE ADJECTIVES

With most adjectives of one syllable, add -*er* + *than*:

> tall → taller than   young → younger than

With one-syllable adjectives ending in -*e*, add -*r* + *than*:

> nice → nicer than   safe → safer than

With one-syllable adjectives ending in one vowel + one consonant, double the final consonant + -*er* + *than*:

> thin → thinner than   big → bigger than

With two-syllable adjectives ending in a consonant + *y*, change the *y* to *i* and add -*er*:

> healthy → healthier than   heavy → heavier than

With two-syllable and three-syllable adjectives, use *more* + adjective + *than*:

> comfortable → more comfortable than   convenient → more convenient than

SUPERLATIVE ADJECTIVES

With most adjectives of one syllable, use the adjective + -est:

tall → the tallest   young → the youngest

With one-syllable adjectives ending in -e, use the adjective + -st:

nice → the nicest   safe → the safest

With one-syllable adjectives ending in one vowel + one consonant, double the final consonant and add -est:

thin → the thinnest   big → the biggest

With two-syllable adjectives ending in a consonant + y, change the y to i and add -est:

healthy → the healthiest   heavy → the heaviest

With two-syllable and three-syllable adjectives, use the most + adjective:

comfortable → the most comfortable   convenient → the most convenient

The following is a list of adjectives that are exceptions. This list must be memorized.

Adjective	Comparative	Superlative
good	better than Kate's grammar is **better than** Judy's.	the best Nora's grammar is **the best** in the class.
bad	worse than Toronto's traffic is **worse than** Calgary's traffic.	the worst Vancouver's traffic is **the worst** in Canada.
far (distance)	farther than Stittsville is **farther** from Parliament Hill **than** Orleans is.	the farthest Smith's Falls is **the farthest** from Parliament Hill.

EXERCISE 1

Fill in the correct comparative and superlative forms of the adjectives in the following chart. Look at the example to help you.

	Adjective	Comparative	Superlative
	short	shorter than	the shortest
1	tired		
2	happy		
3	easy		
4	good		
5	big		

Continued

	Adjective	Comparative	Superlative
6	bad		
7	spicy		
8	peaceful		

EXERCISE 2

Fill in the blanks with the comparative or superlative form of the adjective in parentheses.

The Ottawa Senators are having a _better_ (good) season _than_ the Toronto Maple Leafs.

1. The downtown soccer league is _____ (**expensive**) the one in the suburbs.

2. We hope that tonight's game will be _____ (**short**) yesterday's game.

3. Which of the uniforms at the store is _____ (**cheap**)?

4. Our team is _____ (**competitive**) during home games than during away games.

5. This new baseball bat is _____ (**heavy**) the old one.

6. She is a very good player. In fact, her coach thinks she's _____ (**good**) player on the team.

EXERCISE 3

Fill in the blanks to correctly complete the sentences. Use the words from the list. Note that you will need to change the form of some words. There are more words than sentences. Use each word only once. Look at the example to help you.

~~big~~ beautiful smart clever boring interesting dangerous friendly
good rich poor bad expensive

My car is _____ than yours.   My car is _bigger than_ yours.

1. The weather this summer is _____ than last summer.

2. He is the _____ student in the class.

3. Who is the _____ woman on Earth?

4. This is the _____ class I have ever taken.

5. My dog is _____ than your dog.

6. Living by the ocean is _____ than living in the mountains.

Now, with a partner, compare your answers. Correct your work together.

EXERCISE 4

For each sentence below, identify the adjective. Then use it to fill in the blank, but change it to its correct form—comparative or superlative.

I have an <u>interesting</u> job, but my friend has a _____ job.

I have an interesting job but my friend has a <u>more interesting</u> job.

1. Last night the rain was heavy, but tomorrow it will be much _____ than last night.

2. Josée's apartment is quite expensive, but Marie's is _____ than Josée's.

3. I have a large family, but my grandparents had a _____ family.

4. My marks are good, but Angela's are _____ in the class.

5. Stan's cold is bad today, but tomorrow it will be _____.

6. Georges is a successful writer but his sister is _____ than Georges.

EXERCISE 5

Circle the correct choice to complete the following sentences.

He is _____ his father. (shorter than / the shortest / the most short)

1. Agnes is _____ student in her class. (better / good / the best)

2. My cat is _____ my two dogs. (the youngest / youngest / younger than)

3. These shoes are _____ the black boots. (expensive than / more expensive than / the most expensive)

4. His meal is _____ of all the meals. (hot / the most hot / the hottest)

5. Sam's driving is _____ Maxim's. (badder / worse than / the worst)

6. That statue is beautiful, but the sculpture at the entrance is _____ of the exhibit. (more beautiful than / the beautifulest / the most beautiful)

❖ COMMUNICATIVE ACTIVITY 1

Opinions

Work in pairs. With your partner, talk about three sports or physical activities that each of you has enjoyed doing in the past. Take turns describing each sport or physical activity and compare them with each other. While one person is talking, the other person should write down what his or her partner is saying. Use the adjectives below to help you.

boring	challenging	difficult	easy
good	stressful	satisfying	hard
enjoyable	relaxing	physically demanding	fun

When I was in high school I was on the gymnastics team. I trained on the uneven parallel bars and the trampoline. The trampoline was more fun than the uneven parallel bars. In college I joined the volleyball team; volleyball was more enjoyable than gymnastics. Now I swim for exercise. This is much easier on my joints than volleyball, and it is the best sport for overall toning.

COMMUNICATIVE ACTIVITY 2

World Records Contest

Work in teams. Use a smartphone or other mobile device to find information to fill in the chart below. The teams begin when all are ready. The winning team is the first team to find all the answers and at least one interesting fact about each topic.

	Find . . .	Answer	An Interesting Fact about This Person, Place, or Thing
1	the city with the largest population in the world		
2	the highest point on Earth		
3	the coldest temperature ever recorded		
4	the heaviest animal on Earth		
5	the longest river in the world		
6	the biggest country in the world		
7	the rainiest place on Earth		
8	the most expensive hotel in the world		

	Find . . .	Answer	An Interesting Fact about This Person, Place, or Thing
9	the oldest person in the world		
10	the most visited country in the world		

COMPARATIVE AND SUPERLATIVE ADVERBS

Warm-up

With a partner, look at the two sets of pictures and discuss. Write three sentences of comparison for each set.

_____

_____

_____

_____

_____

_____

Formation

Many adverbs are formed by adding -*ly* to adjectives.

quick → quickly

slow → slowly

Sometimes a letter is changed before adding -*ly*.

happy → happily

comfortable → comfortably

- An adverb is any word or group of words that adds information about a verb. Most adverbs end in -*ly*. We use comparative and superlative adverbs to compare actions.
- When comparing the actions of two people or things, we use the comparative form. When comparing actions of three or more people or things, we use the superlative form.

To form the comparative of adverbs ending in -*ly*, we use *more* + adverb + *than*

To form the superlative of adverbs ending in -*ly*, we use *the most* + adverb

quickly → more quickly → the most quickly

happily → more happily → the most happily

With some short adverbs, we add -*er* to make the comparative and -*est* to make the superlative.

fast → faster → the fastest

loud → louder → the loudest

Some adjectives that end in -*ic* add -*ally*.

scientific → scientifically

academic → academically

genetic → genetically

A few common short adverbs have irregular comparative and superlative forms, which must be memorized.

Adjective	Adverb	Comparative Adverb	Superlative Adverb
good	well I swim well. I draw well.	**better than** Tony swims **better than** I do. Lin draws **better than** I do.	**the best** John Henry swims **the best** of all of us. Vicki draws **the best** of all of us.
bad	badly Reba plays tennis badly. Calum dances badly.	**worse than** Sophie plays tennis **worse than** Reba does. Edmund dances **worse than** Calum.	**the worst** Anna plays **the worst** of all of them. Nate dances **the worst** of all of them.
far	far Bill rode far. We ran far.	**farther than** John rode **farther than** Bill did. The red team ran **farther than** we did.	**the farthest** Alan rode **the farthest** of all. The green team ran **the farthest** of all.

There are also some words that are the same in both their adjective and adverb form.

Adjective	Adverb	Comparative Adverb	Superlative Adverb
hard	hard	**harder than** Elena works **harder than** Max. Oliver tried **harder than** Noah.	**the hardest** Julie works **the hardest** of all. Violet tried **the hardest** of all.
fast	fast	**faster than** My horse runs **faster than** Ryan's horse does. Simon drives **faster than** Luke.	**the fastest** Jean's horse runs **the fastest** of all the horses. Finn drives **the fastest** of all.
early	early	**earlier than** I wake up **earlier than** my son does. We eat dinner **earlier than** our neighbours.	**the earliest** My cat wakes up **the earliest** of all. My grandparents eat dinner **the earliest** of all.

EXERCISE 6

Write the correct comparative and superlative forms of the adjectives in the following chart. Look at the example to help you.

	Adverb	Comparative	Superlative
	quickly	more quickly than	the most quickly
1	safely		
2	beautifully		
3	happily		
4	intelligently		
5	patiently		
6	wisely		
7	carefully		
8	softly		

EXERCISE 7

Fill in the blanks with the comparative or superlative form of the adverb in parentheses.

Jacinthe speaks English (fluent) _____ now than last year.

Jacinthe speaks English <u>more fluently</u> now than last year.

1. This couple dances _____ (graceful) of all the contestants.

2. Planes fly _____ (high) than birds.

3. After his accident last year, he drives _____ (careful) than before.

4. Hank runs _____ (fast) of all the team.

5. Every morning she gets up _____ (early) of her family.

6. They fought _____ (brave) of all of the platoons.

EXERCISE 8

Fill in the blanks with the correct form of the adverb.

Olive swims _____faster_____ than Ryna.   fastest / faster / more faster

1. Of all the students in the class, Roger works _____.
   harder / the hardest / hard

2. On the grammar quiz, I did _____ in the class.
   the most bad / the worst / the baddest

3. I ran _____ than you did.
   more far / farthest / farther

4. She plays tennis _____ of all of us.
   better than / the best / gooder

5. She writes _____ than her sister.
   most careful / the most careful / more carefully

6. Tess sings _____ of all the girls in the choir.
   more beautiful / more beautifully / the most beautifully

7. The team accepted their loss _____ than their coach did.
   more cheerfully / cheerfully / more cheerful

8. Maddie dances _____ of all the ballerinas.
   more graceful / most gracefully / the most gracefully

COMMUNICATIVE ACTIVITY 3

Famous Athletes

With a partner, name three famous athletes from any sports (such as running, hockey, figure skating, tennis, basketball). Compare their abilities. Use these verbs and adverbs:

Verbs			Adverbs		
run	skate	intercept	quickly	fast	straight
swim	throw	race	easily	intensely	effectively
jump	hit	kick	powerfully	successfully	accurately
play	train	catch	defensively		

Usain Bolt is a runner from Jamaica. He ran faster than each of his teammates in the 100-metre race at the 2012 Olympics. He runs the fastest of all the people in the world.

EQUATIVES

Equatives show that certain things and people share the same qualities or characteristics.

Warm-up

With a partner, look at the chart below. Discuss the two things listed in each box.
   Next, write a sentence for each box comparing the two items.

Food	Sports	Activities	Chores	School
pizza	snowboarding	walking	doing laundry	English class
french fries	snowshoeing	shopping	buying groceries	French class

Pizza is not as <u>oily</u> as french fries.

1. Snowboarding is (not) as _____ as snowshoeing.

2. Walking is (not) as _____ as shopping.

3. Doing laundry is (not) as _____ as buying groceries.

4. English class is (not) as _____ as French class.

Formation

Equality and Inequality with Adjectives and Adverbs				
	Keywords	**Use**	**Adjective Examples**	**Adverb Examples**
Equality (of people, things, or actions)	*as . . . as*	expresses the idea of equal, the same as, or similar	Jean is **as athletic as** Robert. Today's earthquake was **as powerful as** the one last year.	Aysen speaks English **as fluently as** Abdul. Joe skates **as fast as** Peter.
Inequality (of people, things, or actions)	*not + as . . . as*	expresses a difference between two people, things or actions	Adults are **not as physically active as** children. Bicycling is **not as dangerous as** skate-boarding.	I do not ski **as frequently as** my brother. I do not read **as effectively** from a computer screen **as** I do from hard copy.

EXERCISE 9

Fill in the blanks to correctly complete the sentences. Use the words from the list. Use each word only once. Look at the example to help you.

quickly	difficult	cold	~~tall~~	quietly	silently	busy	seriously
	proudly	beautiful	old	young	serious		

Suzanne is as _____tall_____ as her daughter.

1. Was the lecture as _____ as it was last year?

2. I want my house to be as _____ as theirs.

3. He went as _____ as he could to the hospital.

4. The lab was not as _____ as the classroom yesterday.

5. The children walked as _____ as mice through the living room.

6. Does she take his ideas as _____ as she does her own?

With a partner, compare your sentences. Correct your answers and then discuss them.

COMMUNICATIVE ACTIVITY 4

Match Game

"Without my glasses, I'm as blind as a bat."

Do you know the expression "as blind as a bat?" What does it mean?

There are several other expressions in English that use "as . . . as."

Your teacher will give you a card. Walk around the room and find the person with the card that matches yours. With your partner, think about what your expression means. In what situation might you use this expression?

BRINGING IT ALL TOGETHER

 COMMUNICATIVE ACTIVITY 5

With your class, choose one of the following topics to debate:

- a two-season climate versus a four-season climate
- living in the country versus living in the city
- cooking for yourself versus eating takeout
- riding a bicycle versus taking the bus
- learning English versus learning another language

Work in teams. Team A is in favour of one of the options; Team B prefers the other. Your teacher will show you how to debate this topic.

Reading

Read the passage and answer the questions that follow.

SHE SHOOTS, SHE SCORES

At the 2002 Winter Olympics in Salt Lake City, the Canadian women's hockey team was the best in the world. They won the gold medal by defeating the United States. These female athletes became instant celebrities and as famous as their male counterparts. This put women's hockey in the spotlight but this achievement was not just confined to the twenty-first century. Women's sports are just as popular in Canada now as they were over 100 years ago. Female hockey leagues were just as popular as male hockey leagues in the province of Quebec at the beginning of the 1900s after Ottawa hosted the first women's hockey game in 1891.

The popularity of women's sports exploded in the 1920s. The women displayed as much strength and <u>stamina</u> as the men and regularly <u>sustained</u> cuts and injuries.

Editorials began appearing more frequently than before in the newspapers, <u>criticizing</u> the physical aspects of the game. If women's hockey was to continue, the players must not bodycheck and the sport must not be seen as rough and as aggressive as men's hockey This behaviour was the most "unladylike" and the most <u>inappropriate</u> of any female sport of the day. This point of view continued through the 1920s and into the 1930s. Sportswriters of the day believed most sincerely that women should only participate in graceful and feminine events that did not involve sweating and getting dirty. This was only an <u>arena</u> for men.

This criticism <u>intensified</u> after World War II. Women had become a more important part of the workforce than men who went overseas to fight. These women produced the manufactured goods required for the war effort. When the war was over, all of the soldiers came home. Women, who were now not as important in the workforce as before, were <u>encouraged</u> to return to the home and their domestic responsibilities. Some women at the time did not like or accept these changes. They felt they were just as <u>viable</u> a part of the workforce as before.

In the 1950s, the most sought-after "feminine traits"—prettiness, daintiness, grace, and a healthy glow—gave a woman social value. Sports reporters would <u>emphasize</u> these feminine traits as the most valued characteristics a female athlete could possess rather than rely on physical <u>accomplishments</u>. The sports that were considered feminine at this time were ice skating, golfing, and swimming. Barbara Ann Scott, Marlene Stewart-Streit, and Marilyn Bell were athletes who most embodied the feminine ideals of these sports. Barbara Ann Scott's femininity was admired for being "doll-like." She had a peaches-and-cream complexion, a rose-bud mouth, and weighed a trim, girlish 48 kilos.

When women began to challenge these ideas in the 1960s and the 1970s, the view of women in sports also began to change for the better. Today, female athletes are described as aggressive, <u>dynamic</u>, powerful, and muscular. They are as capable and as powerful as their male counterparts These female athletes are viewed as physically fit.

<u>Expectations</u> and <u>opportunities</u> for female athletes in Canada have also changed dramatically in the intervening years and, as a result, these female athletes are receiving more positive attention from the media.

Adapted from https://www.historica-dominion.ca/content/education/women-and-sport-footprints-study-guide.

COMPREHENSION

Answer the following questions. Use complete sentences.

1. In 2002, the Canadian women's hockey team was the best in the world. How do we know this?

   _____

2. In the past, women's hockey teams were not as strong as men's teams, and they did not play as hard. True or false? Why?

   _____

3. In the 1920s and 1930s, newspapers told women not to play as hard as men. Why?

_____

4. Who were some of the most admired female athletes in the 1950s? Why did people like them?

_____

5. Which sentence is correct?

Female athletes today are as fit and powerful as male athletes.
Male athletes today are still fitter and more powerful than female athletes.

_____

Listening

🔊 *Track 5*

OUR HOCKEY HISTORY

Listen to the audio.

COMPREHENSION

Answer the following questions. Use complete sentences.

1. What are some of the most popular sports in Canada? Name three.

_____

2. Lacrosse is the most popular winter sport in Canada. True or false?

_____

3. What is Stompin' Tom Connors most famous for?
   a. He wrote one of the most recognized songs about hockey.
   b. He was the best hockey player in Canada in the 1970s.
   c. He once played a home game for the Ottawa Senators.

_____

4. In what year did hockey's most memorable moment take place?

_____

5. Complete this sentence: The most important lessons of sportsmanship are

    _____ and _____.

6. What happened after the McGill University Hockey Club was formed in 1877?

    _____

7. The most prestigious trophy in Canada is the Stanley Cup. Who was Lord Stanley?

    _____

8. Choose the correct answer: When the National Hockey League was formed in 1917, fans were **as loyal / not as loyal** as they are today.

    _____

9. Which Canadian city has Canada's oldest hockey team?

    _____

10. Choose the correct answer: Hockey is becoming **more popular / less popular** in the United States. Explain your answer.

    _____

Writing

Write a short composition (about 200 words) comparing two sports figures. These two people may be famous athletes or two people that you know who excel in their field.

CHAPTER REVIEW

Summary

- There are three basic ways to compare people, places, or things.
- If differences are expressed, then we use comparative or superlative, depending on how many items are being compared.
- The comparative form is used to compare two people, places, things, or actions and uses the word *than*. The comparative can be used with both adjectives and adverbs. The regular comparative is formed with the word *more*:

    more + **adjective** + *than*   *more* + **adverb** + *than*

- Some comparatives use the ending *-er*.

- Some common short adjectives and adverbs have their own irregular comparative form, which must be memorized. The superlative form is used to compare one person or thing with the rest of the group it belongs to. It uses the definite article *the*. The superlative can be used with adjectives and adverbs. The regular superlative is formed with the words *the most*:

    the most + **adjective**   *the most* + **adverb**

- Some superlatives use the ending *-est*.
- Some common short adjectives and adverbs have their own irregular superlative form, which must be memorized.
- The equative form is used to show that two people, places, or things are the same in some way and uses *as . . . as*.

EXERCISE 1

Fill in the blanks with the appropriate comparatives and superlatives to correctly complete the sentences. Use the words from the list. Note that you will need to change the form of some words. There are more choices than sentences. Use each word only once. Look at the example to help you.

good	short	young	comfortable	beautiful	cold	hot	~~sunny~~
	large	interesting	dangerous	bad	far	pretty	lazy

Do you know the _____sunniest_____ place in Canada?

1. My job is _____ than her job.

2. What is the _____ country in the world?

3. I have the _____ drink.

4. My mother is the _____ in her family.

5. Is that table _____ than yours?

6. That is the _____ sofa.

7. Which is the _____ book on the reading list this year?

8. McMillan is the _____ player on the team; the coach needs to talk to him.

9. I like this apartment more than the others, but it's the _____ from my office.

10. This is the _____ dog I know!

EXERCISE 2

Fill in the blanks with the correct form of the words in parentheses. You may need to change the word to an adverb form.

> She jumps **the highest** (high) of all the girls in the school.

1. She plays soccer just as _____ (frequent) as her sister.

2. Sam runs _____ (quick) than any of his teammates.

3. Sidney shoots the puck _____ (aggressive) of all the players.

4. He is _____ (high) scorer in the league.

5. Their team had _____ (bad) results of the season.

6. She won the gold medal for long jump; her jump was _____ (long) than everyone else's.

7. The Chinese team performed their gymnastics exercises _____ (gracefully) than all the other teams.

8. That guy is _____ (dangerous) player on the field; he needs a red card!

9. Kendall danced the routine _____ (beautiful) of all the dancers.

10. We need to practise _____ (hard) if we want to beat the Wolves.

EXERCISE 3

There are seven errors in the following paragraph. Find and correct them. The first one has been done for you.

> the most
> Yesterday's soccer game was ~~more~~ exciting of the season. The Tigers played their
> best game yet. They played best than their opponents and rivals, the Bears, who
> won the soccer trophy last season by beating the Tigers in the final game. The
> Bears controlled the ball more frequent but the Tigers had a better defence. The
> Tigers' defensive players ran fast and had best control over the ball. Their forward,
> Paul Johnson, handled the ball most aggressively than the Bears' forward, John
> Gower, even though John won the trophy for the More Valuable Player last season.
> This season the Tigers just keep playing good than before.

EXERCISE 4

Circle the correct comparatives and superlatives in parentheses in the following letter.

Dear Mom and Dad,

My first day of tennis camp is now over. It was great but it was one of the (more difficult / most difficult) days in my life. The exercises became (harder / hardest) as the day went on. The time did not pass (as quickly / as quicker) as I had hoped. My partner had the same problem but she looked at the time (the most frequently / more frequently than) I did.

I met lots of new people. Some are (more athletic / most athletic) than I am but I am doing as (well / good) as they are. I'm not (more physically fit / most physically fit) than they are, but I am working the (harder / hardest). In the sprints, I ran (as quick / as quickly) as my partner. In one activity we bumped into one another more often (than / then) we liked, but in the end it worked out for the (better / best). I moved the (more carefully / most carefully) of all of the participants because I was nervous about my knee injury from last summer. To injure my knee again would be (worse than / the worst) thing to happen. During the week, I will exercise (more often / the most often) in the pool to strengthen my muscles. The more I look at the week's schedule, the (more excited / most excited) I become.

I hope these two weeks are (better / the best) of the summer! I hope the time passes (most slowly / more slowly) than it did last summer at camp.

Love you!

Amanda

EXERCISE 5

Make sentences to express inequality among people, things, and actions. Insert an appropriate noun or verb in the first blank, and complete each sentence by filling in the second blank with an equative expression from the list.

as easily as	as powerful as	as dangerous as	as quietly as	as carefully as	as playful as

People	_____ are not _____ children.
	_____ does not park _____ my cousin.
Things	_____ are not _____ lawnmowers.
	A _____ does not move _____ a cat.
Actions	_____ is not _____ hang gliding.
	_____ does not come _____ skating for me.

6 The Future

PART 1

1 SIMPLE PRESENT AND PRESENT PROGRESSIVE

2 NOUNS AND PRONOUNS

3 ARTICLES AND DETERMINERS

4 SIMPLE PAST, PAST PROGRESSIVE, *USED TO*

5 COMPARATIVES, SUPERLATIVES, AND EQUATIVES

6 THE FUTURE

OVERVIEW

In English you can express the future four different ways.

Form	Use	Example Sentences
will + base form of verb	<ul><li>for spontaneous decisions (things you decide quickly and carry out immediately)</li><li>for predictions for an uncertain time in the future</li><li>for offers and promises</li></ul>	There's someone at the door. I**'ll see** who it is. Do we need more drinks? I**'ll run** to the corner store. People **will travel** to the moon one day. Someday we**'ll find** a cure for cancer. I**'ll help** you to study for your test. I**'ll carry** your bags for you.
to be going to + base form of verb	<ul><li>for future actions that we intend to do later, usually at a specific time</li><li>for predictions about things that might happen in the near future</li></ul>	She **is going to buy** a car next month. I'm worried about James. I**'m going to talk** to him this weekend. The sky is getting dark. It**'s going to rain**. United are playing well this season. They**'re going to win** the Cup.

Continued

Form	Use	Example Sentences
simple present tense	• for future scheduled events; we need a time marker, such as a day, date, or time Some common verbs with the simple present include *arrive*, *leave start*, *begin*, *end*, *finish*, *open*, *close*, *be*.	The movie **starts** at 8:00 PM tonight. The train **leaves** the station at 7:30 PM tomorrow morning. The mall **closes** at 10:00 PM on Saturday night.
present progressive tense	• for plans that are already arranged We usually know when the event will happen. Time markers (*tonight*, *tomorrow*, etc.) are common.	He **is taking** the plane to Europe tonight. We**'re having** a party tomorrow. I**'m running** in the London Marathon next spring.

Warm-up

Work in pairs. Fill in the chart with plans and predictions about your own life. Share your thoughts with your partner.

	Me	My Family	My City or Community
Tomorrow			It's going to snow!
Next Week			
Next Year	I'm graduating!		
In Five Years			
In Ten Years			

THE FUTURE USING *WILL*

Warm-up

MAKING PREDICTIONS

Work in small groups. What will the world be like in 50 years? Look at the pictures and make predictions about the future. Use *will*.

> I think we will do all of our shopping online.

> I think doctors will find a cure for AIDS.

Share your ideas with your classmates.

Formation

To talk about the future, use the auxiliary *will* + the base form of the verb.

Positive Statement		Negative Statement	
Subject + Auxiliary + Verb (+ object / complement)		Subject + Auxiliary + Negative + Verb (+ object / complement)	
I **will stay** in the city.	I'**ll stay** in the city.	I **will not wait** any longer.	I **won't wait** any longer.
You **will pass** the course.	You'**ll pass** the course.	You **will not know** your results until April.	You **won't know** your results until April.
She **will change** her mind.	She'**ll change** her mind.	She **will not follow** in her sister's footsteps.	She **won't follow** in her sister's footsteps.
It **will go** out of business.	It'**ll go** out of business.	It **will not survive** over the winter.	It **won't survive** over the winter.
We **will get** a transit pass.	We'**ll get** a transit pass.	We **will not see** him again.	We **won't see** him again.
They **will solve** the problem.	They'**ll solve** the problem.	They **will not believe** you.	They **won't believe** you.

We use *will* + the base form of a verb to express the following:

- spontaneous decisions (things you decide quickly and carry out immediately):

  That's okay—don't worry about the spilled coffee. I'll wipe it up.

  The phone is ringing. I'll get it.

- predictions (not immediate, or not specified):

  Traffic will increase in the downtown core, according to the latest survey.

  The Montreal Canadiens will win the Stanley Cup next year.

- offers and promises:

  I will take you to the airport tonight.

  We'll come over and help you cook dinner.

EXERCISE 1

With a partner, use the pronouns in the first column to write positive sentences using *will* + the base form of a verb. Choose a different verb from the list below for each sentence so that each sentence will be different. Then complete the table by writing negative sentences and yes / no questions. Look at the example to help you.

get married   catch   hear   know   begin   throw   shut   see   speak
pay   wear   strike   fight   feel   bite   deal   fall

Positive Statement	Negative Statement	Yes / No Question
Subject + Auxiliary + Verb (+ object / Complement)	Subject + Auxiliary + Negative + Verb (+ object / complement)	Auxiliary + Subject + Verb (+ object / complement)
I'll get married in a few years.	I won't get married in a few years.	Will I get married in a few years?
You		
He / She		
It		
We		
You		
They		

EXERCISE 2

Which use of *will* is shown in the sentences below? (Circle) the correct answer for each sentence.

1. I'll call the hotel tomorrow and book us a room.

   spontaneous decision / prediction / promise or offer

2. The dog needs to go out. I'll take her for a walk.

   spontaneous decision / prediction / promise or offer

3. Call me when you arrive, and I'll pick you up at the bus station.

   spontaneous decision / prediction / promise or offer

4. One day, no one will read books; everything will be electronic.

   spontaneous decision / prediction / promise or offer

5. Let me help you. I'll get the door for you.

   spontaneous decision / prediction / promise or offer

6. I expect I'll get married eventually, but not yet.

   spontaneous decision / prediction / promise or offer

EXERCISE 3

Andy and Susannah are getting married next summer. Today they are dreaming about their future life together. Change each of the following sentences to a wh- (information) question you could ask them. The information you want to ask about is **bolded** and underlined.

We'll both get **big promotions at work**.

What will you both get?

1. We'll buy **a beautiful house in the suburbs**.

   _____?

2. We'll go to our cottage at the lake **every summer**.

   _____?

3. Our children will go **to the best schools**.

   _____?

4. We'll spend our weekends **gardening or doing home improvements**.

   _____?

5. <u>Our son</u> will score the winning goal in the Stanley Cup final.

_____?

6. We'll never fight <u>**because we love each other**</u>.

_____?

EXERCISE 4

Look at the pictures. What is each person saying? Finish the sentences.

There's nothing for dinner. I'll go to the store.

1. Don't worry, Mom. I _____

_____

2. It's okay, sis. I _____

_____

3. One day _____

_____

4. I promise I _____

_____

5. Maybe in the future _____

_____

✸ COMMUNICATIVE ACTIVITY 1

It's Not Happening!

Work with a partner. Look at the verbs and time expressions on the following page.

Student A: Choose one of the verbs, and make a positive sentence in the future (*will* + base verb). Use one of the time expressions. Do not contract the verb!

Student B: You think your partner is wrong! Use the same verb and time expression to make a negative sentence. Contract the auxiliary *will* + *not*.

Take turns until all verbs are used.

A: Next week Susan will win the lottery.

B: Next week Susan won't win the lottery.

begin	go	forget	fly	drive	eat	break	hide	feel
know	~~win~~	sleep	sell	fall	wear	teach	think	

this afternoon	~~next week~~	this weekend	next semester	the day after tomorrow
tonight	after class	next month	in a few minutes	

⚡ COMMUNICATIVE ACTIVITY 2

Predictions

Work with a partner. Look at these three situations. What do you think will happen to these people in the future? What will happen to them next year, in five years, and in ten years? Share your predictions.

Patricia, 27

I can't believe it. After eight years as an administrative assistant with the same company, I found out yesterday that I'm losing my job. I'm upset, but I have a dream. I want to open an online store. I want to design and sell colourful and stylish office accessories: mouse pads, folders, storage boxes, that kind of thing. I have no business experience, but tomorrow I'm meeting someone at the bank to ask about a business loan.

JJ Cool Dude, 23

Life is pretty good right now! I grew up in a rough part of town and I didn't have cool clothes or electronics. Sometimes I didn't have enough to eat. Music was my life, and I started to write and sing rap songs when I was 12. I love how I feel when I'm making music. I'm playing in nightclubs in the city and my fans love me. Tomorrow I'm meeting someone from a recording company. I'm going to be a star!

Carly, 18

I applied to five universities, but I am not interested in any of them. I don't want to go to university and sit in a lecture room. I want to see the world. I want to get a job on a cruise ship, either in the restaurant or as a lifeguard at the pool. I'll meet lots of interesting people, and I'll save some money. My parents aren't going to be happy, but tomorrow I'm telling them I'm not going to university.

THE FUTURE USING *BE GOING TO*

Warm-up

Look at the sentences below. For each plan, make two predictions. One should be optimistic; the other should be pessimistic.

> I'm going to spend next summer backpacking around Europe.
>
> > You'll meet lots of interesting people.
> >
> > You'll run out of money.

1. Nancy is going to apply to medical school.

   _____

   _____

2. Will is going to adopt a stray dog from the animal shelter.

   _____

   _____

3. My parents are going to retire to the south of France.

   _____

   _____

4. Your own plan:

   _____

   _____

   Your predictions:

   _____

   _____

Formation

To express future actions that are already planned, use a form of *be going to* + the base form of the verb. *Be going to* + the base form of a verb expresses the idea that something is certain to occur (a prediction) because of an existing plan or proof (for example, tickets purchased, reservations made).

In spoken English, the subject pronoun and the verb *be* are often contracted in both positive and negative sentences.

Positive Statement		Negative Statement	
Subject + Auxiliary + Verb (+ object / complement)		Subject + Auxiliary + Negative + Verb (+ object / complement)	
You **are going to win** the Speaking prize.	**You're going to win** the Speaking prize.	You **are not going to believe** the news.	**You're not going to believe** the news.
She **is going to ask** her parents for help.	**She's going to ask** her parents for help.	She **is not going to call** her ex-boyfriend.	She **isn't going to call** her ex-boyfriend.
It **is going to snow** all night.	**It's going to snow** all night.	It **is not going to rain** tomorrow.	It **isn't going to rain** tomorrow.
We **are going to visit** friends in Victoria.	**We're going to visit** friends in Victoria.	We **are not going to give** you another chance.	**We're not going to give** you another chance.
They **are going to move** house in the summer.	**They're going to move** house in the summer.	They **are not going to give** her any more money.	**They're not going to give** her any more money.

When using a form of *be going to* in spoken English, the verb is contracted. Often it can sound like "gonna" (as in "I'm gonna go to the movies") but *gonna* is not a proper word, so it should not be used in writing.

EXERCISE 5

Work in pairs. Use the pronouns in the first column to write positive sentences using the correct form of *be going to* + the base form of a verb. Choose a different verb from the list below for each sentence so that each sentence will be different. Now complete the table by writing the negative sentences and questions. Look at the example to help you.

~~ride~~	give	watch	succeed	call	win	have
fight	blow	drink	buy	teach	shake	run

Positive Statement	Negative Statement	Yes / No Question
I am going to ride the roller coaster.	I am not (I'm not) going to ride the roller coaster.	Are you going to ride the roller coaster?
You		
He / She		
It		
We		
You		
They		

EXERCISE 6

Read the following paragraph about Tina.

Last semester Tina found her courses difficult. She was taking an extra course, so she had more work than usual. She had a part-time job in a fast-food restaurant, and she worked there for 20 hours each week. On top of that, she usually went out on weekends with her friends. She stayed out late on Saturdays, and she slept all day on Sundays. She also had a boyfriend. She spent at least two hours every day calling him and texting him. For these reasons, Tina didn't devote enough time to studying, and she almost failed four of her courses. Yesterday, Tina spoke with her academic advisor. She wants to make some changes.

What is Tina going to do next semester? How is her life going to be different? Write six sentences about Tina. One suggestion is given here.

She is going to quit her part-time job.

_____

_____

_____

_____

_____

EXERCISE 7

Fill in the blanks with _going to_ + a verb from the list. Contract the verb each time. Look at the example to help you.

| ~~move~~ | reserve | cook | load | bring | help | drive | spend | drive |

We**'re going to move into** a new apartment next month. On moving day, we _____ the moving van, and then Mark _____ the van to the apartment building. I _____ our car, and I _____ Rex the dog with me. We _____ the service elevator from 9:00 AM to 10:00 AM to get our furniture into the apartment. Our friends will be there too. They _____ us carry the heavy furniture. We _____ the rest of the day unpacking and organizing our apartment. At the end of the day, we _____ dinner in our new apartment.

COMMUNICATIVE ACTIVITY 3

I'll Check My Calendar

Your calendar is very full! Look at each of these events. For each one, decide what you are going to (a) wear, (b) eat, (c) buy, and (d) do. Use "be going to _____" for each of the four sentences for each event. Try to use a different verb for each sentence.

1. your best friend's wedding

2. a weekend camping trip

3. your grandmother's birthday

4. your own upcoming event!

EXPRESSING THE FUTURE WITH THE SIMPLE PRESENT TENSE

Warm-up

With a partner, write five sentences in the simple present tense using the following information. Look at the example to help you.

The <u>bus</u> <u>arrives</u> <u>at 8:00 PM.</u>

~~bus~~	end	~~at 8:00 PM~~	semester
movie	leave	Monday	begin
class	start	tonight	September
train	~~arrive~~	noon	

_____

_____

_____

_____

_____

Formation

We can use the simple present to refer to scheduled future events. To indicate that these events are in the future, the sentence will often contain a time marker—for example, "tomorrow at noon," or "tonight at 8:00 PM."

The new school semester starts in August next year.

The plane leaves at 8:00 AM Friday morning.

Remember that the third person singular in the present tense ends in *-s*.

EXERCISE 8

Write six other time markers not mentioned above.

_____

_____

_____

_____

EXERCISE 9

Change each of the following sentences to a wh- (information) question. The information you want to ask about is **bolded** and underlined.

Her plane leaves for Mexico **tonight at midnight**.

When does her plane leave for Mexico?

1. The boat arrives from Kingston **tomorrow morning**.

   _____?

2. The school semester ends **on April 30**.

   _____?

3. The play starts tonight **after the reception for the director**.

   _____?

4. The opera finishes **at 11 o'clock**.

   _____?

5. The sun rises **tomorrow morning at 5:57**.

   _____?

EXERCISE 10

Change the sentences from the previous exercise into the negative.

Her plane leaves for Mexico **tonight at midnight**.

Her plane does not (doesn't) leave for Mexico tonight at midnight.

_____

_____

_____

_____

_____

EXPRESSING THE FUTURE WITH THE PRESENT PROGRESSIVE TENSE

Warm-up

Think about your week. Write down four things that you plan to do and when you plan to do them. With a partner, compare and discuss your plans.

Formation

The present progressive is formed with the verb *be* (in the present tense) and the present participle of the base verb (the *-ing* form). We use the present progressive to express a planned event in the future.

EXERCISE 11

Fill in the blanks with the present progressive tense of the verbs in parentheses.

He **is attending** (attend) a seminar at the college tonight.

1. We _____ (go) to the union meeting after class today.

2. He _____ (fly) to Cuba at 8:00 PM tomorrow.

3. They _____ (study) English later this afternoon.

4. Karl _____ (repair) his car after dinner tonight.

5. We _____ (paint) the kitchen tomorrow after breakfast.

EXERCISE 12

Below is a chart that shows Martin's schedule for the weekend. Use the present progressive to write sentences about Martin's weekend.

◀	Day	**Week**	Month	▶

Saturday	Sunday
9:00 AM — work at grocery store	8:00 AM — go to the gym
3:00 PM — shop for groceries	11:00 AM — meet friends for brunch
5:00 PM — prepare dinner	2:00 PM — study at the library
7:00 PM — watch movies	8:00 PM — take time to relax

On Saturday Martin is working at the grocery store at 9:00 AM.

____

____

____

____

COMMUNICATIVE ACTIVITY 4

My Week

Complete the following chart in point form with things that you are doing in the next week. Use the present participle (base + *-ing*) of each verb.

◀	Day	**Week**	Month	▶

	Day	Evening
Monday		
Tuesday		
Wednesday		
Thursday		
Friday		
Saturday		
Sunday		

With a partner, discuss your plans based on what you have written in the chart.

Now, exchange your books and write a short composition about your partner's plans (aim for 150 to 200 words). Use the present progressive tense.

Read your composition to your partner. Have your partner check for any errors.

BRINGING IT ALL TOGETHER

 ## COMMUNICATIVE ACTIVITY 5

Vacation Time

You have booked a five-day holiday at the Azul Resort in Cuba. Read the poster below and in the chart, write the things that you plan to do while you are there.

Beachfront Resort
Azul, Cuba

All inclusive resort—meals and beverages
All the amenities

No service charge for activities!
- snorkelling, scuba diving
- parasailing, water skiing, wakeboarding
- fishing, boat tours of nearby attractions
- golf, horseback riding
- Latin dance lessons
- Pilates and yoga every morning

- **Beach Café** serving breakfast & light lunch
- **Sunset Bistro** serving eclectic fare and traditional Cuban dishes
- **Azul Restaurant**—fine dining Cuban style—dine and Latin dance under the stars
- **Coco Bar**—local musicians and a floor show every night
- Daily bus tours to Havana and a stop at the local artisan market

	Day	Evening
Monday		
Tuesday		
Wednesday		
Thursday		
Friday		

With a partner, discuss the activities you have planned. Use *going to* + verb. Give reasons why you have chosen these particular activities.

Now, exchange books with your partner and write a short composition (150 to 200 words) detailing what your partner will do on his or her holiday in Cuba. Read each other's paragraphs aloud. Review the various ways you expressed the future in your writing and how you used time clauses and time markers. Help each other correct any errors.

Reading

Read the news item and answer the questions that follow.

THE AGE OF SPACE FLIGHT BEGINS

Nathaniel Kang, 17, already knows what he wants for his eighteenth birthday. This technology-crazy teenager is part of a growing number of citizens who have set their travel sights farther than Florida or Hawaii. If Nathaniel gets his wish, his future trips will be into outer space.

Regular citizens like Nathaniel are soon going to be able to travel to outer space, thanks to the Xcor Lynx Space Flight Rocket. This small rocket is making space travel <u>accessible</u> to ordinary people; all you need is the <u>means</u> to pay for a ticket.

It will be a journey like no other. After take-off, the Xcor Lynx will climb at a 75-degree angle. When the rocket is flying in space, it will reach the maximum speed of Mach 2.9 or 3,550 kilometres per hour. It will break the <u>sound barrier</u> 58 seconds after it takes off.

After three minutes, the Lynx spacecraft will be 58 kilometres from Earth. The engine will switch off, but the rocket will still travel fast enough to reach the maximum distance of 100 kilometres from Earth in about 1.5 minutes. When passengers look out the window of the rocket, the view of Earth will be <u>stunning</u>. Astronauts say that this view of Earth changed their lives.

The Lynx flights are starting soon. The first flight departs later this year, but unfortunately, Nathaniel will not be on it. The cost for this <u>unforgettable</u> experience is $95,000 US, and Nathaniel's parents don't have that kind of money. Still, Nathaniel is <u>optimistic</u>. "I guess I'm getting socks or something for my birthday," he says. "But I'm going to save my money, and I'm sure prices will come down. One day, I'll be in that rocket!"

Adapted from http://www.flyfighterjet.com/xcor-lynx-space-flight/?gclid=CLWKlbbf77QCFao7MgodiV8ApQ.

COMPREHENSION

Answer the following questions. Use complete sentences.

1. Where will Nathaniel's future trips take place?

   _____

2. What are ordinary citizens soon going to be able to do?

   _____

3. How fast will the Xcor Lynx Space Flight Rocket travel?

   _____

4. At what point will it break the sound barrier?

   _____

5. How far away from Earth will the rocket be in 4.5 minutes?

   _____

6. When does the first flight depart?

   _____

7. What does Nathaniel guess he is getting for his eighteenth birthday?

   _____

8. What is Nathaniel going to do, to make sure his dream comes true?

   _____

ANALYZING THE READING PASSAGE

Find and circle all the time markers in the news item.

Listening

🔊 *Track 6*

ON THE WAY TO THE RESORT

Two friends, Camille and Farah, are at the airport. They are getting ready to board their plane to go on holiday for a week.

Part 1

Listen to the audio. Then answer the following questions.

1. Where are Camille and Farah going on holiday?

   _____

2. When is the plane leaving?

   _____

3. What gate will Camille and Farah go to?

   _____

4. How long is the flight to Jamaica?

   _____

5. How long is the bus ride from the airport in Jamaica to their resort?

   _____

6. How many restaurants are at the resort?

   _____

7. Write down four activities that Camille and Farah are going to do or sports they are going to play.

   _____

Part 2

Listen to the conversation again. Write down the activities that are available at the resort. This will include the available day trips. Write a short composition (maximum 150 words) about the activities you would like to do on a vacation to this resort. Use the future tense and try to include future time clauses.

Writing

Read the following poster. It outlines the events that are scheduled for the Spring Tulip Festival on May 21 and May 22. Decide which events you will attend. Then write a short email to a friend who used to live in your town (maximum 150 words) about what you are planning for the weekend. Use different ways to express the future.

Spring Tulip Festival, Saturday May 21 & Sunday May 22

OPEN-AIR FARMERS' MARKET AT THE TIN HOUSE COURTYARD
Stock up on local organic produce, locally made sausage, preserves, pickles, maple syrup, and more!
Saturday 8 AM to 4 PM and Sunday 8 AM to 4 PM

ARTISANS UNDER THE CANOPY IN MAJOR HILL PARK
For Sale: sculpture, jewellery, furniture, clothing, and more.
Saturday 10 AM to 6 PM and Sunday 10 AM to 6 PM

CUNDELL'S HAYRIDES   Ride starts and ends at the Centre Square.
Tour the Old Town Market in a horse-drawn wagon (20-minute tour).
Donations for Humane Society accepted.
Saturday 11 AM to 3 PM and Sunday 11 AM to 3 PM

CONCERT IN THE PARK — FREE!   Major Hill Park
The Street People Band will do a Beach Boys tribute. Bring a picnic and a blanket.
Saturday 7 PM to 10 PM

FAMILY 3K WALK TO BENEFIT HUMANE SOCIETY
Registration per family: $5.00
All proceeds go to the Humane Society.
Donations are welcome.
Start: Conference Centre Sunday at 7:30 AM **End:** Pretoria Bridge
Buses available to return to Conference Centre.

CHAPTER REVIEW

Summary

There are four ways in English to express the future.

1. Simple future tense: *will* + the base form of the verb

2. *to be going to* + the base form of the verb

3. Simple present tense (often used with schedules—e.g., for transportation)

4. Present progressive tense (used for plans already made for the near future)

EXERCISE 1

Change each of the following sentences into a yes / no question.

We're flying to Montreal tonight. → Are you flying to Montreal tonight?

1. I'll answer the phone.

   _____?

2. One day, I will travel in outer space.

   _____?

3. Your father will help you with your résumé and job application.

   _____?

4. I will try to confirm your reservation.

   _____?

5. We're going to stay at a campsite on the beach.

   _____?

6. I'm going to major in Dance at college.

   _____?

7. The game starts at 7:30.

   _____?

8. Their flight arrives at Terminal 2 at 10:48.

   _____?

9. Emma and Sophie are coming to my birthday party!

   _____?

10. Next semester, we're both taking Ancient Civilizations.

   _____?

EXERCISE 2

Rewrite the following paragraph, changing the past tense verbs to the future (*going to* + base form of the verb). Look at the example to help you. There are seven more verbs to change.

Last year we went on a ski trip to Mont Tremblant. We stayed in a condo at the base of the mountain. The package included the lift ticket and breakfast. We ate breakfast in the restaurant at the top of the mountain Saturday and Sunday morning. We took the gondola up in the morning because it was cold. After a day of skiing, we enjoyed après-ski in one of the bars at the foot of the mountain. We had a great weekend.

Next year we are going to go on a ski trip to Mont Tremblant. _____

_____

_____

_____

_____

_____

_____

_____

_____

EXERCISE 3

Change each of the following sentences to a wh- (information) question. The information you want to ask about is **bolded** and underlined

Karl is going to write **his exam** tonight. → What is Karl going to write tonight?

1. We are catching the flight to **New York**.

   _____?

2. They are going to study grammar **at the library**.

   _____?

3. He will get lost **because he does not have GPS in his car**.

   _____?

4. I am going to put **gas** in the car.

   _____?

5. She will spend all her money on **clothes and shoes**.

   _____?

6. They are going to wash the dishes **after dinner**.

   _____?

7. The company is going to give **a bonus cheque** to each employee.

   _____?

8. I'm leaving **at seven o'clock** tomorrow morning.

   _____?

9. Our train departs from **Platform 4**.

   _____?

10. The wedding starts **at six o'clock**.

   _____?

EXERCISE 4

In the following passage describing the future, fill in each blank with the correct form of the verb in parentheses. There may be more than one possible answer.

Space travel _____ (become) a popular type of vacation in the future, and space travellers _____ (need) to think carefully about their health. Some doctors are already planning for this development.

Dr. Ted Cook of Edmonton is one such doctor. "I _____ (take) a course in space-age medicine next year," he says. "Some of my younger patients _____ (want) to travel beyond the Earth, and we need to be prepared." Dr. Cook's course _____ (start) in January and _____ (include) topics like motion sickness and the effect of radiation on the human body. "I know I _____ (learn) a lot," he says.

There is still a lot that doctors don't know about the effect of space travel on the body. "People _____ (stay) in space hotels for long periods of time, and we don't know how that _____ (affect) their health," says space scientist Dr. Victoria Khan. "The next few years _____ (be) very important in the development of our understanding."

Part 1 Review

Self-Study

PART 1

1 SIMPLE PRESENT AND PRESENT PROGRESSIVE

2 NOUNS AND PRONOUNS

3 ARTICLES AND DETERMINERS

4 SIMPLE PAST, PAST PROGRESSIVE, *USED TO*

5 COMPARATIVES, SUPERLATIVES, AND EQUATIVES

6 THE FUTURE

OVERVIEW

The self-assessments in this unit give you a chance to review and reinforce the grammar points from Part 1 (Chapters 1–6). Check your knowledge, and if you find areas that need more attention, go back to the appropriate chapter and review the material.

EXERCISE 1

Fill in each blank with the correct form of the verb *be*. Pay attention to the keywords or phrases.

1. Today there _____ many dogs in the park.

2. Last night there _____ a thunderstorm.

3. _____ you _____ at school tomorrow?

4. He _____ not happy with his shoes; his feet are hurting.

5. _____ there a car in the driveway yesterday?

6. I _____ at the pharmacy right now.

7. Later this afternoon we _____ in class.

8. They _____ not _____ ready for the trip tomorrow.

9. We _____ not with him last night.

10. It _____ ready for us next week sometime.

- The simple present tense describes facts and habits. The key words that indicate the simple present are adverbs and expressions of frequency.
- The present progressive tense uses the *-ing* form of the verb and describes an action that is happening in present time. The key words or phrases that indicate the present progressive are adverbial phrases such as *today, at this moment, this week*.

EXERCISE 2

Fill in the blanks using the simple present tense or the present progressive tense. Pay attention to the keywords.

Yolanda always _____ (wear) casual clothes to school. She usually _____ (prefer) jeans, T-shirts, and hoodies. Today, however, she _____ (wear) a smart business suit and high heels. After class she _____ (have) a job interview with the campus communications office. Yolanda _____ (take) courses in journalism this year, and she _____ (want) to work in public relations. Right now, Yolanda _____ (sit) in her class, feeling quite uncomfortable!

EXERCISE 3

Change each of the following sentences into a yes / no question.

1. He goes to the market every Saturday.

   _____?

2. This semester, we are taking a self-defence course.

   _____?

3. They are happy to volunteer after school.

   _____?

4. The teacher is speaking too quickly right now.

   _____?

5. We want to see the movie.

   _____?

6. She is taking her car to the garage right now.

   _____?

EXERCISE 4

Change each of the following sentences to a wh- (information) question. The information you want to ask about is underlined.

1. We need to send the information immediately.

   _____?

2. The soup is hot.

   _____?

3. We meet our friends for coffee every morning.

   _____?

4. They are late because the car broke down.

   _____?

5. He is putting flowers on the head table.

   _____?

6. I ride a bike in the summer.

   _____?

EXERCISE 5

Unscramble the following groups of words to make negative sentences.

1. is not travelling / my family / right now / in Europe

   _____

2. his bike / Vincent / to class / does not ride / in winter

   _____

3. a long time / it / to get downtown / does not take

   _____

4. do not use / I / to get / the bus / to work

   _____

5. to walk / Sarah / does not want / after dinner

   _____

6. is not wrapping / right now / my gift / my sister

   _____

EXERCISE 6

Fill in the blanks with the plural form of the noun in parentheses.

1. Who are the two _____ (woman) over there?

2. I am dating Steve, but I like Paul! I need some _____ (advice)!

3. Fiona doesn't mind History, but _____ (Sociology) is her favourite subject.

4. We're having 250 people at the wedding, including 12 _____ (child) and
   3 newborn _____ (baby).

5. Plant the tree in the hole, then fill in the hole with _____ (soil).

6. Shall we have _____ (pasta) for dinner tonight?

7. How much _____ (time) do you have? I need some help.

8. How many _____ (time) did you call her?

EXERCISE 7

Find and correct the nine pronoun errors in the following passage.

Two years ago, mine family went on a trip. It was their first family vacation. We were very excited. Your sister and I packed our suitcase by themselves. My mother helped my father pack his. Us left in the morning and reached our destination, Wonderland, at four o'clock. Mine parents checked into our hotel. My sister and I unloaded the car by ourselfs and took the bags to the room. We spent two action-packed days at Wonderland. My father went on the rollercoaster by hisself because my mother, my sister, and I were too afraid. Dad said it was the best experience of him life. We tried all of the rides and had a great time. Family vacations are amazing!

EXERCISE 8

Fill in the blanks with *a*, *an*, *the*, or *some*. If no word is needed, write Ø. There may be more than one correct answer.

I enjoy planting _____ garden in the spring. I like to plant _____ flowers in the front garden. I have _____ small herb garden in the backyard. I do not plant _____ tomatoes in the garden, but I have them in pots on _____ back deck. In the summer I often go to _____ farmers' market in _____ town. I like to buy _____ fruit and vegetables there because everything is fresh.

EXERCISE 9

Find and correct the errors for *this*, *these*, *that*, and *those* in the following passage.

Fashion has not changed much throughout time. Look at this pants. Those was the style 10 years ago and now it is in style again. My mother wore that shoes when she was married. In a shoe store today, you can see those same style of shoe.

EXERCISE 10

The simple past tense describes actions that started and finished in the past.

Yesterday at noon, a fire broke out in the cafeteria, but the fire department quickly put it out.

The past progressive tense refers to past actions that occurred at specific past time.

Yesterday, at noon, we were eating lunch in the cafeteria.

Complete the following sentences using either the simple past or the past progressive tense.

1. Last night we _____ (watch) the news on television.

2. Last week he _____ (finish) the project.

3. Yesterday we _____ (study) in the library at two o'clock.

4. A week ago it _____ (rain) in the mountains.

5. Two days ago at 8:00 AM she _____ (swim) in the pool.

EXERCISE 11

Change each of the following positive sentences into the negative.

1. My uncle was driving dangerously on the highway.

   _____

2. I rode my bicycle to school every day last year.

   _____

3. We left the city before rush hour.

   _____

4. That elderly man was standing on the bus when I got on.

   _____

5. We slept on the plane last night.

   _____

EXERCISE 12

Change each of the following sentences from the simple past to *used to* + the base form of the verb, to indicate a past habit.

1. When my mother was young, she went to a lot of parties.

   _____

2. As a child, I took swimming lessons.

   _____

3. While Alan was in high school, he played soccer.

   _____

4. When my son was a teenager, he stayed up late.

   _____

5. During university, Karl ate his meals at the cafeteria.

   _____

EXERCISE 13

Find and correct the error in each of the following sentences.

1. Some people believe the wealthy have more better lives than the middle class.

   _____

2. When she was a child, she got sick more easy than her sisters.

   _____

3. That song is popular as this one. _____

4. I am tallest than my sister. _____

5. When he was a child he ran most quickly than his brother.

   _____

EXERCISE 14

You can express the future in four different ways in English. Write an example sentence for each of the four forms in the following chart.

Use	Form	Example Sentences
spontaneous and voluntary actions and predictions	*will* + base form of verb	
future actions that are already planned	*be going to* + base form of verb	
future scheduled events Uses the verbs *arrive, leave, start, begin, end, finish, open, close, be.*	simple present tense	
plans that are already arranged	present progressive tense	

EXERCISE 15

Rewrite the following pairs of sentences as one sentence using a time marker.

when	before	after	as soon as	unless	until

1. Sophie will save her money. Then she will buy a car.

   _____

2. Alan will graduate in the spring. Afterwards he will look for a job.

   _____

3. James will return from teaching in France this September. He will apply for a teaching position in Saudi Arabia in October.

_____

4. I will drive my sister to the airport first. I will take the car to the garage afterwards.

_____

5. Mara's sister will help her pack on Saturday. On Sunday Mara will leave for New York.

_____

EXERCISE 16

Change each of the following sentences to an information question. The information you want to ask about is underlined.

1. The most popular girls' names in Canada are Emily, Olivia, and Maya.

_____?

2. Real Madrid won the big soccer match last night.

_____?

3. Stefan was suspended from the college because he plagiarized an assignment.

_____?

4. I downloaded an app about English grammar.

_____?

5. We're staying at the Palace Hotel, near the cathedral.

_____?

6. Leah went to China three years ago.

_____?

7. You should back up your files every day.

_____?

8. They saved $10,000 by not eating out and not buying electronics.

_____?

Combining Clauses

PART 2

7 COMBINING CLAUSES

8 PRESENT PERFECT

9 MODALS

10 TYPES OF QUESTIONS AND SHORT ANSWERS

11 PREPOSITIONS AND PHRASAL VERBS

12 PAST PERFECT AND CONDITIONALS

OVERVIEW

- Clauses are parts of sentences. An independent clause (IC) is one complete sentence with a subject and verb and perhaps an object. A dependent clause (DC) also contains a subject and a verb. It adds information to an independent clause, but it cannot be a sentence on its own because it doesn't express a complete thought.

- Sentences that contain two clauses are either compound or complex.

  - A compound sentence contains two independent clauses (IC + IC):

    We travelled to South America, and we spent one week in Lima.

    Independent Clause   Independent Clause

  - A complex sentence combines an independent clause with a dependent clause. The independent clause could come first (IC + DC):

    We visited the Monastery of San Francisco while we were in Lima.

  - or the dependent clause could come first (DC + IC):

    While we were in Lima, we visited the Monastery of San Francisco.

    Dependent Clause   Independent Clause

- A sentence that has more than one clause needs the correct punctuation and connecting word to make the clauses into one complete sentence.

- We can connect clauses with coordinating conjunctions, conjunctive adverbs, relative pronouns that serve as conjunctions, and subordinating conjunctions.

COORDINATING CONJUNCTIONS

Warm-up

Work in groups of three. Imagine you have all just met at a party and you want to get to know each other.

Student A: ask a question from the list below to Students B and C.

- What do you like to do on the weekends?
- What sport do you like to watch?
- What is your favourite colour?
- What kind of music do you like to listen to?

Students B and C: Reply to Student A with information about yourself.

Student A: Make a sentence about both students, using either *and* or *but*.

Switch roles and play three rounds, giving everyone a chance to be Student A.

Student A: What do you like to do on the weekends?

Student B: I like to play soccer.

Student C: I like to go to the movies.

Student A: You like to go to the movies, but you like to play soccer.

Formation

Conjunction	Example Sentence
for	I wouldn't try to change her mind about staying, **for** it is too late. She has already left.
and	She is taking singing lessons, **and** she has started to take dancing too.
nor	He doesn't enjoy sports, **nor** does he like music. He prefers to read all the time.
but	I have no cash on me right now, **but** I have my credit card.
or	You can call me collect, **or** you can text me on my cellphone.
yet	She doesn't own a computer, **yet** she is very knowledgeable about computers.
so	The roads were icy this morning, **so** I drove to school very carefully.

Coordinating conjunctions connect two independent clauses to make a compound sentence.

The Eiffel Tower is a famous tower. It is in France.

Independent Clause   Independent Clause

We can combine these two clauses with *and*:

> The Eiffel Tower is a famous tower, and it is in France.

You can also use a different conjunction, *but*, in a different sentence:

> The Eiffel Tower is a famous tower, but it is not the tallest in the world.

There are seven coordinating conjunctions. We sometimes use the acronym FANBOYS to remember them.

F	A	N	B	O	Y	S
for*	and	nor	but	or	yet*	so

*Note: *For* and *yet* are not common in conversation; you are most likely to see them in written English.

There is usually a comma (,) before a FANBOYS conjunction when you are joining two independent clauses, unless both clauses are very short:

> IC + comma + FANBOYS conjunction + IC

EXERCISE 1

Circle the best conjunction to complete each of the following sentences.

1. Teresa remembered to bring her umbrella, (or / but / for) she forgot to wear her raincoat.

2. I came home late, (so / yet / and) I ordered a pizza for dinner.

3. It is 3:00 in the morning, (but / and / nor) I haven't finished writing my essay.

4. This scarf is beautiful, (but / for / yet) it is very affordable.

5. You can live in a student residence, (and / or / yet) you can rent an apartment; it's your choice.

6. Sebastian lost his bus ticket and wallet, (nor / or / but) he managed to get home somehow.

EXERCISE 2

Connect each of the following pairs of sentences using a FANBOYS conjunction. You may have to rewrite some sentences and there may be more than one correct answer.

1. She is frequently late for work. She still managed to get a promotion.

   _____

2. The musicians rehearsed the song many times. They kept stumbling over one note.

   _____

3. It is warm and sunny today. The forecast promises more sunny days for this week.

   _____

4. I withdrew extra money from the bank. I won't run out of money this time.

   _____

5. Can you use chopsticks? Do you prefer a knife and fork?

   _____

CONJUNCTIVE ADVERBS IN COMPOUND SENTENCES

Conjunctive adverbs connect two independent clauses to create a compound sentence:

   IC + conjunctive adverb + IC = compound sentence

There are many different ways to connect the ideas expressed in the two independent clauses. For example, some conjunctive adverbs which do the connecting show similarity, while others may show contrast or provide additional information.

Formation

Below is a chart of the most commonly used conjunctive adverbs. Refer to Appendix B for more examples.

Purpose	Conjunctive Adverb	Example Sentence
to give more information	in addition	Cars are becoming more expensive to purchase; **in addition**, gas prices are continually on the rise.
	furthermore	Too much pollution is adding to our waste-management problems; **furthermore**, our climate is showing some drastic changes as well.
	moreover	The students have a lot of assignments this week; **moreover**, they are preparing for their midterms next week as well.
	besides	She is a good speaker. She is the natural selection for class representative; **besides**, she really wants to do the job.
to give an example	for example	Puccini wrote some of the world's most famous operas; **for example**, *Tosca* and *Madama Butterfly* are both well worth seeing.
to show a result	therefore	Banks are closed on Labour Day; **therefore**, your week's pay will be deposited the next day.

Purpose	Conjunctive Adverb	Example Sentence
to show something unexpected	however	He is going on holiday for a month; **however**, he is bringing his tablet and will stay in touch with the office by email.
to show a contrast	on the other hand	The scenic route by train is pretty; **on the other hand**, the plane gets us there sooner.
to show emphasis	in fact	He needs to have his surgery sooner than we imagined; **in fact**, he should book an appointment as soon as next week.
to correct someone	actually	The correct answer to the math question isn't 26. **Actually**, it's 27.

When a conjunctive adverb connects two clauses into one sentence, it is preceded by a semicolon (;) and followed by a comma (,):

Hardcover books are becoming more and more expensive; **however,** if you wait for the paperback edition, you can save money and still enjoy owning the book.

The relationship between two sentences can also be shown by beginning the second sentence with a conjunctive adverb, followed by a comma (,).

Hardcover books are becoming more and more expensive. **However,** if you wait for the paperback edition, you can save money and still enjoy owning the book.

EXERCISE 3

Circle the best connector to complete each of the following sentences. Add punctuation as needed.

1. Consider the damages of the oil spill in the sea; (moreover / actually / in fact) consider the damages to the birds and other wildlife.

2. The boxes are all ready for the move; (on the other hand / therefore / besides) the suitcases are not packed yet.

3. The tropical cruise is a great idea for this time of year; (on the other hand / moreover / therefore) we'd get to see whales if take the Alaska cruise instead.

4. You should eat less fast food; it has a lot of grease. (Furthermore / Besides / Actually) you shouldn't be consuming too much salt anyway, and fast food has a lot of salt.

EXERCISE 4

Write your own compound sentences using the connectors below. Look at the example to help you.

_____ ; moreover, _____

The bus to the airport was late; moreover, the subway was delayed.

1. _____; therefore, _____

_____

_____

2. _____; however, _____

_____

_____

3. _____; in fact, _____

_____

_____

4. _____; actually, _____

_____

_____

5. _____; besides, _____

_____

_____

RELATIVE PRONOUNS AS CONJUNCTIONS

Relative pronouns are used to connect adjective clauses to the rest of the sentence. An adjective clause identifies or modifies a noun, giving more information about it.

I know the man **who delivers our pizza**.

The adjective clause "who delivers our pizza" gives more information about the noun *the man*.

The relative pronoun *who* connects the adjective clause and the main clause.

The choice of relative pronoun depends on its function in the sentence and to what it is referring.

Formation

Relative Pronoun as Subject		
Refers to a . . .	**Pronoun**	**Example Sentences**
person	who / that (informal)	The hockey player **who** was born in Russia is my favourite. The hockey player **that** was born in Russia is my favourite.
thing	which / that	We saw a movie **which** appealed to both of us. We saw a movie **that** appealed to both of us.
Relative Pronoun as Object		
Refers to a . . .	**Pronoun**	**Example Sentences**
person	whom (formal) / that / Ø (no pronoun)	That is the woman **whom** I saw at the movies. That is the woman **that** I saw at the movies. That is the woman I saw at the movies.
thing	which / that / Ø (no pronoun)	He read the book **which** I left on the table. He read the book **that** I left on the table. He read the book I left on the table.
Relative Pronoun as a Possessive		
Refers to a . . .	**Pronoun**	**Example Sentences**
person	whose	The woman **whose** children were causing a disturbance left suddenly.
thing	whose	The house **whose** roof had blown off was not fit for sleeping in.

That can often replace *who, whom,* or *which.*

When the relative pronoun is an object, we can omit *whom, that,* or *which.*

When combining these two sentences with the same subject, we omit one subject:

The Eiffel Tower is a famous tower. ~~The Eiffel Tower~~ is in France.

Now add a connector:

The Eiffel Tower is a famous tower *that* is in France.

When the relative pronoun is the object, it can be omitted.

The Eiffel Tower is the famous tower I saw in France.

EXERCISE 5

Circle the best relative pronoun to complete each of the following sentences.

1. That is the same book (**who / that**) was recommended to me.

2. Chocolate is the one snack (**who / that**) almost everybody loves.

3. People (**which / who**) are always late really annoy me.

4. Teachers appreciate students (**who / whom**) ask questions in class.

5. The jeans (**who / Ø**) I bought yesterday are too small.

6. That's the guy (**what / who**) borrowed my phone and didn't return it!

7. The woman (**whose / who's**) children I babysit is having another baby.

8. Have you seen the coffee cup (**Ø / whose**) I left here five minutes ago?

EXERCISE 6

Connect each of the following pairs of clauses with the best choice of relative pronoun.

The family just got a new dog. The family lives next door to me.

The family that lives next door to me just got a new dog.

1. The teddy bear is for his baby sister. He bought the teddy bear from a gift shop.

   _____

2. She got the chocolate bar from the corner store. She is eating the chocolate bar.

   _____

3. The new books are all in English. The library ordered the new books.

   _____

4. The basketball team is on the train. The train is arriving at the station.

   _____

5. The man was driving his car. His car broke down last week.

   _____

6. The movie was a James Bond movie. We saw it last night.

   _____

INDEFINITE PRONOUNS AND ADJECTIVE CLAUSES

Warm-up

Your teacher will show you some pictures of people and things. With a partner, try to guess who or what each picture is.

I think she's **someone who** owns a business.

I think he's **somebody who** has been in jail.

I think it's **something that** we use in the kitchen.

Formation

Adjective clauses can also modify indefinite pronouns in a sentence, as shown in the following chart.

Indefinite Pronoun	Example
one	This is the one **that I was telling you about**.
someone	Give it to someone **who can look after it**.
somebody	The prize should go to somebody **who deserves it**.
something	This is something **that is worth paying for**.
other(s)	These are the books that the others **left behind**. The red pen is the other pen **that the teacher gave me**.
another	This is another slice of pizza **which has more pepperoni on it**.

There are two types of adjective clauses: identifying and non-identifying.

Identifying adjective clauses give essential information about the noun.

My brother who lives in Tokyo works for an IT company.

In this sentence, "who lives in Tokyo" is essential information. It tells us *which* brother works for an IT company; maybe the speaker has several brothers, and we need this information to be clear about the identity of the IT worker.

Non-identifying adjective clauses give non-essential information about the noun. This type of adjective clause can be omitted from the sentence without changing the meaning of the rest of the sentence or making the making the identity of the noun unclear. It is set off by two commas (,).

My brother, who lives in Tokyo, works for an IT company.

In this sentence, "who lives in Tokyo" is non-essential information. We already know which brother the speaker means; the fact that he lives in Tokyo is not crucial for us to identify him.

Proper punctuation is important when writing non-identifying clauses. The non-essential information is enclosed by commas (,).

EXERCISE 7

Decide which of the following sentences have **identifying** adjective clauses and which have **non-identifying** ones. Write "**I**" for essential information and "**NI**" for non-essential information in the blank after each sentence.

The gentleman who is wearing a white bow tie is the bridegroom.   I

The gentleman, who is wearing a white bowtie, is the bridegroom.   **NI**

1. The coffee shop that is across the street is closed today. _____

2. The cream dress, which my grandmother wore for her wedding in 1945, now belongs to my mother. _____

3. The email that was marked "urgent" went into my spam folder. _____

4. My colleague whose wife left him is now living with his mother. _____

5. The song that I was telling you about earlier won the Grammy Award. _____

6. Write down the phone number of the doctor, whose name I keep forgetting, in your daily planner. _____

⁙ COMMUNICATIVE ACTIVITY 1

People I Know

Work in pairs. Think of five people you know in your life and draw each of them in the following chart. Now describe them to your partner using relative pronouns.

This is my neighbour who lives next door to me. She is a 67-year-old woman who loves to sit on the porch in front of her house.

Picture	Description (This is _____ who / that _____.)

SUBORDINATING CONJUNCTIONS IN COMPLEX SENTENCES

An independent clause (IC) is one complete sentence with a subject and verb and perhaps an object. A dependent clause (DC) also contains a subject and a verb. It adds information to an independent clause but cannot be a sentence on its own because it doesn't express a complete thought.

Subordinating conjunctions connect a dependent clause to an independent clause to form a new complete sentence called a complex sentence.

> She was late because she missed the bus.

In this sentence, "She was late" is the IC. It can exist alone, without the DC. The DC is "because she missed the bus." It cannot exist alone; something is missing.

ICs and DCs are connected with subordinating conjunctions. Some of the more common subordinating conjunctions are *when*, *because*, *although*, *before*, *after*, and *if*.

I met my best friend **when** I was in elementary school.
     IC   DC

We became friends **because** we have the same interests.
     IC   DC

We keep in touch **although** we no longer live in the same city.
     IC   DC

When using subordinating conjunctions, you have two options:

IC + DC (She was late because she missed the bus.)
DC + IC (Because she missed the bus, she was late.)

There is no real difference in meaning, but note the difference in punctuation.

In the first sentence, the independent clause (IC) comes first, so no punctuation is needed before the dependent clause (DC). In the second sentence, where the DC comes first, we need a comma (,) before the IC.

Formation

The following are some of the most common subordinating conjunctions. Please see Appendix C for more examples.

Purpose	Subordinating Conjunction	Example Sentences
to show a time relationship	before after when whenever while until as soon as	He didn't study **before** he wrote the test. I'll buy a new suit **after** I get my paycheque. I'll call you **when** I arrive at the bus station. I go shopping for new clothes **whenever** I am in London. I saw a big dog **while** I was walking in the park. You need to practise this piece of music **until** you can play it perfectly. I called my parents **as soon as** I got my exam results.

Continued

Purpose	Subordinating Conjunction	Example Sentences
to show a purpose	so (that)	I came to Montreal **so (that)** I could learn French.
to show a reason	because as	I need to clean my apartment **because** I'm having friends for dinner. Leo can't come **as** it's a holiday in his culture.
to show an unexpected event	although even though	I want to stay up and watch the movie **although** it's late and I'm tired. He passed his driving test **even though** he didn't stop at a red light!
to show a condition	if even if unless	We can get the 9:20 train **if** we take a taxi to the station. You can't pass the course **even if** you get 100 percent in everything from now on. We won't get a refund **unless** we return the items soon.

EXERCISE 8

Match the following dependent and independent clauses. Fill in the blanks with the letter of the correct independent clause from the second column.

1. After we eat breakfast, _____

2. Even though we're late, _____

3. Unless we put it on a credit card, _____

4. When you find an apartment, _____

5. While you were away, _____

6. Although I already have eight other pairs of designer jeans, _____

7. Because you have a terrible sense of direction, _____

8. Even if you have enough cash, _____

a) I bought a new pair.
b) we can't afford to buy it.
c) it's a good idea to take a couple of credit cards as well.
d) we can go to the mall.
e) we can still catch the early show.
f) I strongly recommend you take a GPS with you.
g) I fed your cat and watered your plants.
h) you must send us your new address.

EXERCISE 9

In the following sentences, two of the three options are suitable; the other one is not. Circle the two possible subordinating conjunctions to complete each sentence, and discuss with your class why the third option is not correct.

1. (**As soon as / When / Because**) I get a new job, I will have a party to celebrate.

2. Lorenzo got a red card (**because / before / after**) he kicked another player in the knee.

3. Don't forget to turn all the lights off (**although / when / before**) you go to bed.

4. We can't go skiing (**until / when / unless**) we get more snow.

5. It feels like autumn (**before / as / because**) all the leaves are changing colour.

6. (**Although / Because / Even though**) she was not a strong student in high school, she went to university and became a successful CEO.

BRINGING IT ALL TOGETHER

 ## COMMUNICATIVE ACTIVITY 2

Plan the Perfect Day

Amy, Sandi, Cass, Lenny, and David were friends in college and graduated in the same year. Ten years later, they are meeting up again to spend a day together. Look at the possible events below and the friends' profiles on the next page, and in groups, decide how they should spend their day. Your choices don't need to be limited to the advertised events; you may have a better idea! The friends don't need to all be together, all of the time.

Grand Opening! ***Franz's Fish Fiesta*** The best seafood in the northern hemisphere Open from 12:00 PM to 11:00 PM *Free drink to first 100 customers!*	*Now on at the City Art Gallery* **The Art of the Pre-Raphaelites** A stunning collection of rarely seen oil paintings from Europe. Open all day; free admission	*For one night only!* 𝔐𝔬𝔫𝔰𝔱𝔢𝔯 𝔐𝔢𝔱𝔞𝔩 Canada's favourite heavy metal band in concert Saturday, 9:00 PM For tickets, call 555-6732 𝔇𝔬𝔫'𝔱 𝔪𝔦𝔰𝔰 𝔦𝔱!
Learn to ballroom dance Introductory lesson only $25. Saturday, 4:00 PM–6:00 PM Singles welcome. Call 555-9021 for details.	**International Cheese Festival** Sample up to 12 different cheeses from France, Italy, and Germany. Special event at Victoria's Rare Books. Admission $55.	*Saturday Soccer* See the ***Smallville Saints*** in a once-in-a-lifetime exhibition game against ***Manchester United***! Kick off at 3:00 PM Tickets limited—hurry!

Suggested language you can use:

There are two people who don't like _____.

They can't go to _____ because _____.

After they _____, they can _____.

_____ can go to _____ while _____ and _____ go to _____.

Because only _____ likes _____, they need to _____.

Amy		Full-time mom to four-year-old Tyler, who will come with her. Enjoys all kinds of music; hates shopping. Has severe allergies to some foods, including dairy products.
Sandi		Editor for a literary magazine; single. Likes quiet places, such as libraries and museums; dislikes sports. Uses a wheelchair.
Cass		Unemployed; lives with her boyfriend, who plays in a punk band. Likes shopping, loves restaurants, enjoys most sports. Likes to stay out late and dance the night away.
Lenny		Engineer; married with three children, but will come alone. Loves sports; doesn't enjoy the arts or literature. Currently has his right arm in a cast after a soccer accident.
David		IT consultant; engaged to Melissa, who will come with him. Both enjoy fine dining, wine tasting, designer shopping, and the opera. Both go to the gym every day.

Reading

Read the article and answer the questions that follow.

FRIENDSHIP

What is the new meaning of "friendship" these days? One would think that the word *friend* or the concept of friendship should never change through the passage of time, but somehow it seems to have <u>evolved</u> in the last few years. How many friends do you have? When it comes to having friends, is it the <u>quality</u> or the <u>quantity</u> of the friendships that is more important?

Consider the word *friend* that we use on <u>social networks</u>. Are all of those people really our friends, or a mix of relatives, friends, and acquaintances? Maybe they are even people we have never met in person whom we have befriended online. Many live in faraway places which we may never even have the opportunity to visit anytime soon.

Perhaps we can use new words to describe the new types of friends we have these days.

Cyber friend or social network friend: This is a friendship that we have initiated online, and which continues to exist online. It consists of frequent or occasional dialogues that can be of serious or casual nature. It may even consist of a simple exchange of comments or photographs related to a subject of common interest.

Buddy: Buddies are close friends whose personal information we are well aware of. We know their full names; we know where they live; we have a generally good idea of their likes and dislikes, and we like to hang out with our buddies, or do particular activities together such as play soccer or meet for a drink on a regular basis.

Bosom buddy: A bosom buddy is a term that hasn't been used in recent years. Your bosom buddy is your closest friend and confidant. It is someone you feel the closest to and with whom you share your most private thoughts. The origin of the term *bosom buddy* may date back to times when a mother shared her breast milk with another child who wasn't her own, and the two children grew up to be very close, like a family.

BFF: BFF stands for "Best Friends Forever" and is a new term used these days. As we know, very few friends last the test of time. We can grow apart and develop different interests, which can put a strain on the friendship. So, in essence, your BFF is your closest friend and has been your closest friend for a very long time, which is the reason for the use of the word *forever*.

Pal: *Pal* is another name for friend, but it isn't used that often except perhaps in anger to a stranger: "Listen, pal!" However, in the pre-computer days, the term *pen pal* was very popular. We could connect to someone whose home was in a faraway land or <u>exotic</u> country and write to them for many, many years. We would exchange cultural information and learn about each other's lives and send pictures. With the speed of email, many of these "snail mail" habits are disappearing, unfortunately.

Continued

Acquaintance: Now we get to the word that you should actually use for many of your "friends." An <u>acquaintance</u> is someone whose name you know, and whom you have met on a number of occasions, but whom you really don't know very well. We have to know others well to love them, trust them, and to give them the title of "friend." It takes time and effort for both you and your friends to earn that title in each other's opinions. However, feelings can sometimes be hurt if we consider someone an acquaintance, and he or she considers us a friend.

So, the next time we are introduced as someone's friend, we should really ask ourselves, "What type of friends are we?" or "How well do we know each other?" to really understand the relationship. Let's ask ourselves again: how many friends do we *really* have?

COMPREHENSION

1. For each definition in the second column, write the letter of the corresponding term in the first column.

    a) Cyber friend   _____ someone who lives far away and who sends letters to you

    b) BFF   _____ someone who hears all your secrets

    c) Bosom buddy   _____ someone you like to socialize with

    d) Pen pal   _____ someone you know through Facebook or Twitter

    e) Acquaintance   _____ someone whose friendship you will treasure forever

    f) Buddy   _____ someone you are friendly with but don't know well

Answer the following questions.

2. What is the difference between a "buddy" and a "bosom buddy"?

    _____

3. How is the word *pal* often used today?

    _____

4. What word should you really use for most of your "friends"?

    _____

ANALYZING THE READING

Read the article again and (circle) all the relative pronouns.

DISCUSSION

1. Can you be friends with a person whom you have never met face to face?

2. How can you tell when an acquaintance has become a friend?

3. Has your definition of the word *friend* changed after reading this article? If so, how?

Listening

🔊 *Track 7*

MEMORIES OF SUMMER CAMP

Listen to the audio. Indicate whether the following statements are true (T) or false (F); circle the correct letter.

1. All three are happy to be reunited.	T	F
2. There are lots of people at this reunion.	T	F
3. Marla is a violinist.	T	F
4. It was easy to recognize everyone at this reunion.	T	F
5. Soha always helped Marla with her tray when they used to camp together.	T	F

COMPREHENSION

Listen to the audio again and answer the following questions. Write complete sentences.

1. After how many years are these friends reunited?

   _____

2. What did Eve call Soha for one entire summer?

   _____

3. What detail about one summer do they keep referring to?

   _____

4. Who is Jimmy Nilsson?

   _____

5. How is Soha paying the price for that hot summer?

   _____

Writing

Write a short composition (250 words) about the pros and cons of eating at a restaurant rather than at home. Use arguments about healthy diet, cost, and social setting.

_____

_____

_____

_____

_____

_____

_____

_____

_____

CHAPTER REVIEW

Summary

- Connectors bring two ideas together. Coordinating conjunctions and conjunctive adverbs can connect two independent clauses.

- Relative pronouns and subordinating conjunctions connect dependent and independent clauses.

- Relative pronouns (*who*, *that*, *which*) connect dependent clauses to independent clauses.

- Relative pronouns connect adjective clauses to independent clauses.

- Coordinating conjunctions (FANBOYS) connect two independent clauses.

- Conjunctive adverbs (such as *therefore*, *however*, *in fact*) are preceded by a semicolon (;) and followed by a comma (,) to connect two independent clauses.

- Subordinating conjunctions (such as *because*, *after*, *before*, *since*) connect ideas within sentences.

EXERCISE 1

Write sentences about your own life, using the connectors provided. You will need to add the correct punctuation to your sentences.

_____ moreover _____

I want to go into nursing when I graduate because I'm interested in health science; moreover, I enjoy working with people.

1. Although _____

2. _____ however _____

3. _____ besides _____

4. Because _____, I _____

5. When _____, _____

EXERCISE 2

Fill in the blanks with a suitable word. There may be more than one correct answer.

1. It is better to eat a piece of fresh fruit than to drink juice _____ there is less sugar in fresh fruit.

2. _____ you decide to become a vegetarian, it is often a good idea to take a multi-vitamin pill.

3. Some experts recommend drinking eight glasses of water each day, _____ others say that is not necessary.

4. Tofu, _____ is made from soya beans, is now a very popular food item in Western countries.

5. There are some diet books _____ recommend not eating meat and potatoes in the same meal.

6. The man _____ book encourages readers to eat like cavemen is now a millionaire.

7. _____ too much alcohol is considered dangerous, there is evidence that an occasional glass of red wine can be healthy.

8. You shouldn't eat cake, cookies, or chocolate when you are trying to follow a healthy diet; _____, burgers and fried chicken should be limited.

9. _____ you are in a restaurant, you should choose a large salad as your main course.

10. You can have your salad with meat, _____ you can have it with cheese or eggs. It's up to you.

Present Perfect

PART 2

7 COMBINING CLAUSES

8 PRESENT PERFECT

9 MODALS

10 TYPES OF QUESTIONS AND SHORT ANSWERS

11 PREPOSITIONS AND PHRASAL VERBS

12 PAST PERFECT AND CONDITIONALS

OVERVIEW

We form the present perfect by using the present tense of *have* + the past participle of the verb. The present perfect has three main uses in English. In all three uses, it gives us a way to connect or create a link among past, present, and potential future actions.

The main three uses of the present perfect in English are to express

1. indefinite or unspecified past actions

    I have been to China.

2. actions started in the past and continuing in the present (duration)

    I have lived here for three years.

3. repeated past actions.

    I have eaten pasta three times this week.

Warm-up

Walk around the classroom and interview four students. Ask the following questions and record answers in the table. At the end of the exercise, share your findings with the rest of the class.

	Use 1	Use 2	Use 3
	Have you ever received an A in any courses? Which ones?	How long have you been a student here?	How many times this term have you been to the library to do homework?
1			
2			
3			
4			

PRESENT PERFECT: INDEFINITE OR UNSPECIFIED PAST

INDEFINITE OR UNSPECIFIED PAST

We use the present perfect when we ask about past actions. We don't know if those actions actually occurred in the past, or when they occurred. We often use words like *ever*, *yet*, and *already* with these questions.

We also use the present perfect when we are talking about our own past experiences, but do not say when or how often our experiences took place. As soon as we give a time expression, we need the simple past.

Warm-up

Work in pairs. Read the following conversations out loud.

CONVERSATION 1

Have you ever been to Toronto?

Yes, I have been to Toronto before. I'm from Montreal. Have you ever visited Montreal?

No, I have never visited Montreal, but I have always wanted to.

CONVERSATION 2

Have you seen the new James Bond movie yet?

No, I haven't seen it yet. Let's go see it this weekend.

CONVERSATION 3

Have you given a speech in English recently?

Yes, I have. I gave one last week. I have never acted in an English play; have you?

CONVERSATION 4

Have you already graduated?

No, I haven't, but my sister has just graduated. She graduated last week.

Look again at each conversation. Which tenses are used in each one? Can you see a difference between the uses of tenses?

Formation

Look at the warm-up conversations again. We don't know the exact timing of the actions, or even whether they happened.

Use	Form	Keywords	Example Sentences
unspecified past	*has / have* + past participle	ever	Have you **ever** been to Italy? (lifetime experience)
		never	No, I've **never** been there. (lifetime experience, negative form)
		always	No, but I've **always** wanted to go. (constant or ongoing wish)
		recently	Yes. We have **recently** come back from Italy. (It happened a very short time ago.)
		already	Yes. I've **already** been to 12 countries in Europe. (It happened, but no time is given.)
		yet	I haven't been there **yet**—one day! (I am expecting to go.) I've
		just	**just** booked a trip to Italy! (It happened a short time ago.)
		lately	Have you been anywhere **lately**, or are you still staying close to home?
		Note: There may be no keyword.	

Note: You CANNOT use the present perfect with specific time expressions such as *yesterday, one year ago, last week, when I was a child, when I lived in Poland, at that moment, that day, one day*, and so on. Look at these example dialogues.

Have you sold your house yet?

Yes, we sold it *last week.*

Have you ever been in a talent competition?

Yes, I have. I was in one *when I was a child.*

Refer to Appendix A to see a list of all irregular past participles.

Look at the warm-up conversations again. Notice the placement of the keywords.

Have you <u>ever</u> visited Montreal?

No, I have <u>never</u> visited Montreal, but I have <u>always</u> wanted to.

Have you seen the new James Bond movie <u>yet</u>?

No, I haven't seen it <u>yet</u>.

Have you given a speech in English <u>recently</u>?

Have you <u>already</u> graduated?

No, I haven't, but my sister has <u>just</u> graduated.

> The keyword can come either before the past participle or at the end of the sentence.

EXERCISE 1

Are the verb tenses in the following sentences correct or incorrect? If a tense is incorrect, say why, and then write the correct tense.

1. I've been to Thailand in 2005.

   _____

2. Zara's grandparents immigrated to Canada in 1968.

   _____

3. Did you ever meet a famous movie star?

   _____

4. Daniel always wanted to go to New York, and now he's going!

   _____

5. I have never been in a hot air balloon.

   _____

6. We've been on a cruise to the Caribbean last winter.

   _____

EXERCISE 2

Fill in the blanks using the present perfect form of the verbs in parentheses.

1. Do you know Frank? No, I _____ (meet, not) him yet.

2. Sam _____ (see, already) the new exhibit at the museum.

3. _____ (receive, you, ever) an email like this one? I think someone is trying to scam me.

4. We _____ (be, never) to an NHL game. Have you?

5. _____ Marie _____ (find out) about the surprise party yet?

6. Let's try that new pizza place. _____ (try, you) it yet?

7. _____ (hear, you, ever) about the free trips for students through that agency?

8. Fantastic! I'm in. I _____ (have, never) a helicopter ride before.

EXERCISE 3

Work in pairs. Answer these questions with short answers. If you answer "yes," tell your partner about the event.

Have you ever seen the movie *Transformers*? → Yes, I have. / No, I haven't.

Have your parents been to Canada? → Yes, they have. / No, they haven't.

1. Have you ever won a contest?

2. Have you ever had a really bad haircut?

3. Have you ever scored 100 percent on a test?

4. Have you moved out of your parents' home yet?

5. Have you read any of the Harry Potter books in English?

6. Have you ever been to an NHL game?

COMMUNICATIVE ACTIVITY 1

Pair Work

Read the following dialogue. Where do you think this conversation is taking place?

A: Marco, have you ever worked in a restaurant?

B: Yes, I have. When I was in high school, I worked in a fast-food restaurant. I served customers and cleared tables.

A: Have you ever cooked food in a restaurant?

B: No, I haven't, but I like cooking. I often cook meals for my family.

A: And have you ever been fired, or had a problem with a manager?

B: No, I haven't. I get along well with people.

Now, work in pairs. One of you is a candidate for a part-time job; the other is the interviewer.

Look at the list of jobs below. Talk about them. What skills are needed for each job?

- server in a restaurant
- telemarketer
- tour guide in a museum
- lifeguard at a swimming pool
- cashier in a busy supermarket

Interviewer: Decide which questions to ask. What past experience or previous education should the candidate have?

Candidate: Consider how best to talk about your skills. For example, if you *have* done something, you should then tell the interview where and when you did it. If you *have never* done something, what can you say instead?

When you have finished, change roles!

PRESENT PERFECT: PAST TO PRESENT

A CONNECTION TO THE PRESENT

We use the present perfect when we're talking about an action that started in the past and is still true today. There is a good chance that this action will continue into the future.

Warm-up

Read the following passage and underline the verbs in the present perfect tense.

Hi. My name is Martin. I'm a student. I have lived in Vancouver for the last six months. I moved here in the summer. I have studied computer engineering at the college since September. So far, I have learned a lot and I have received excellent marks on my assignments. A lot of what we have studied until now has been theory. However, in the last two weeks, we have started to apply that theory. I have found that I now understand the theory a lot better. I have heard that the activities in the labs become even more practical next semester, so I'm really looking forward to the next three semesters.

Formation

Use	Form	Keywords	Example Sentences
an action that started in the past and is still true today	has / have + past participle	how long . . . ? for since until now so far how often . . . ? how many times . . . ?	**How long** have you worked here? I have worked here **for** three years. I have worked here **since** 2002. I've worked here **from** last winter **until** now. I've worked here **for** two years **so far**.

FOR OR *SINCE*?

Use **for** with an amount of time (i.e., how long):

I have lived here for three years.

She has studied at this college for two terms.

They have been married for 20 years.

Use **since** with a specific point in time (i.e., when the action started):

I have lived here since I came to Canada.

She has studied at this college since last September.

They have been married since 1994.

EXERCISE 4

For each question, decide if the sentence refers to an amount of time or to a specific point in time. Fill in the blank with *for* if it is an amount and *since* if it is a specific point in time.

1. Where were you? I have been here _____ five hours!

2. I have been allergic to milk _____ I was born.

3. I've listened to your music _____ 60 seconds, and I already have a headache!

4. His plan to retire isn't a secret. I've known about it _____ a long time.

5. We've known each other _____ July 15. We met at a wedding.

6. I've been home _____ 11:00 AM, but no one has called me.

7. I've been on a diet _____ the holidays, but I haven't lost any weight!

8. Joe has been unemployed _____ two months, but he has an interview tomorrow.

EXERCISE 5

Use the present perfect of the verb in parentheses in the first blank and *since* or *for* in the second blank.

1. We _____ (be) here _____ two hours.

2. She _____ (speak) French _____ she was young.

3. He _____ (know) Catherine _____ three years.

4. I _____ (study) harder for my exams _____ I got that failing grade.

5. I _____ (have) my driving permit _____ six months.

6. He _____ (wear) glasses _____ he was 10 years old.

7. She _____ (smoke) _____ she was 16.

8. They _____ (enjoy) skateboarding _____ several years.

THE PRESENT PERFECT PROGRESSIVE TENSE

In some cases, you will see sentences that look like this:

How long have you been working here?

I have been working here since 2002.

How long have they been living there?

They have been living there for 10 years.

The present perfect progressive is formed with *have / has* + *been* + the base form of the verb + *-ing.* We use it to emphasize a continuing action. There is no real difference in the meaning between the present perfect and the present perfect continuous, or progressive.

You can usually only use a progressive tense with **action verbs**.

EXERCISE 6

In the following passage, all of the present perfect verbs have been <u>underlined</u>. Change them to the present perfect progressive, if possible. Remember there are some verbs that can't be used in that way.

Hi. My name is Martin. I'm a student. I <u>have lived</u> in Ottawa for the last six months. I moved here in the summer. I <u>have studied</u> computer engineering at the college since September. So far, I <u>have learned</u> a lot and I <u>have received</u> excellent marks on my assignments. A lot of what we <u>have studied</u> until now <u>has been</u> theory. However, in the last two weeks, we <u>have started</u> to apply that theory. I <u>have found</u> that I can now understand the theory a lot better. I <u>have heard</u> that the activities in the labs become even more practical next semester, so I'm really looking forward to the next three semesters.

COMMUNICATIVE ACTIVITY 2

Jane Doe's Life Timeline

Jane Doe was born in 1990. The timeline below shows the dates Jane started doing important activities in her life. She still does all these activities.

1. Make two sentences for each activity using the present perfect and the present perfect progressive. The first sentence will use *since* and the second one will use *for*. The first set has been done for you as an example.

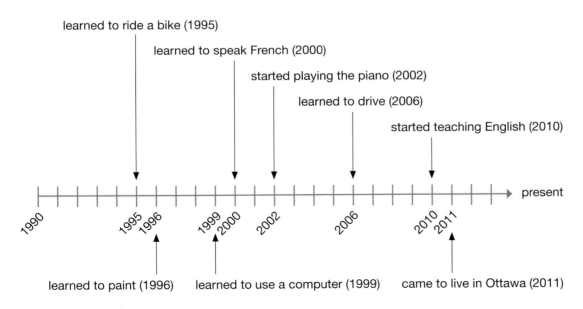

learned to paint (1996)

Jane has painted since 1996.

Jane has been painting for 18 years.

2. Ask a friend questions about Jane's timeline using *how long* or *how many years.*

   How many years has Jane painted? OR How many years has Jane been painting?

COMMUNICATIVE ACTIVITY 3

My Life

1. Look again at Jane Doe's timeline. You are going to make your own timeline. In the timeline below, fill in the correct years. Then add some events in your own life.

year you were born   present

2. Now work in groups. Share your timeline with your group. Take turns asking and answering questions about your life.

PRESENT PERFECT: REPEATED PAST ACTIONS

We use the present perfect to describe actions that have occurred in the past at different or repeated times.

Warm-up

Find someone in your class who . . .

has eaten lots of junk food lately.	has frequently been to dance clubs.	has been to a coffee shop every day this week.
has written several poems or stories.	has often thought about moving to a new country.	has had a few part-time jobs.
has changed his or her mind about something many times.	has taken the bus more than three times this week.	has taken more than one course in computer skills.

Formation

Use	Form	Keywords	Example Sentences
repeated past actions	*has / have* + past participle	twice, three (four, five, etc.) times several times many times a few times how often . . . ?	I **have been** to Europe twice. I enjoyed it **both times**. They **have eaten** at this restaurant **several times**. She **has explained** this **many times**.

EXERCISE 7

Work in pairs. Ask each other the following questions.

How many times have you used Google this week?

I have used Google three times this week. OR I haven't used Google this week.

1. How many times have you played a computer game this week?

2. How often have you tweeted this week?

3. How many pictures have you uploaded to Facebook this week?

4. How many friend requests have you accepted this week?

5. How often have you found a homework answer online this week?

6. How many online groups have you contributed to this week?

7. How many songs have you downloaded this week?

8. How many texts have you sent this week?

COMMUNICATIVE ACTIVITY 4

Can You Help Me, Nurse?

Work in pairs. One partner is a nurse, while the other is a patient who is addicted to his or her smartphone. Read the following dialogue and decide what each person says. Use your imagination!

Patient: Can you help me, nurse? I'm addicted to my phone. I've had a smartphone for three years now, and I can't stop using it. I've tried everything, but nothing has worked.

Nurse: What kinds of _____?

Patient: Well, so far this week, I've _____, I've _____, I've _____, and I've _____.

Nurse: I see. What have your friends and family said about this?

Patient: My mother has told me _____. My friends have _____.

Nurse: Has your daily life changed since you got a smartphone?

Patient: Yes. I used to _____, and now I don't do that. I've stopped _____, and I've lost _____.

Nurse: Have you ever tried _____?

Patient: _____.

Nurse: All right. What you should do is _____ _____.

Share your conversations with the class.

BRINGING IT ALL TOGETHER

COMMUNICATIVE ACTIVITY 5

Excuses!

Work in groups of four. Role-play the following situations. Each of you has been let down by three people. However, they all have excuses. Listen to the excuses your group members provide, and decide which one is best. Look at the example to help you.

Example situation: You are a boss. Three of your employees are late for work, and they all look as if they haven't slept. They all have excuses.

Person A. "I've been chasing a mouse since two o'clock this morning. It's been running around my house! I still haven't caught it."

Person B. "My parents are visiting on the weekend. I haven't cleaned my house for six months. I've been cleaning since midnight."

Person C. "I've been looking after my cat all night. She's going to have kittens. Would you like one?"

Situation for Student A: You have invited several people for a formal dinner. Three of them arrive late. They are not dressed up, and they haven't brought wine or flowers.

Situation for Student B: You are teaching an evening course for adult students. This week, three students have not done their homework.

Situation for Student C: You are spending the term in another country. Your best friends have been ignoring you; you haven't heard from them for two months. Suddenly, you receive three very apologetic emails.

Situation for Student D: It was your birthday yesterday. Three of your best friends forgot about it. Today, you see them at your school.

COMMUNICATIVE ACTIVITY 6

Conduct a Survey

Interview at least 10 people using the following questions.

	1. What is the best movie you have ever seen?	2. How many times have you seen it?	3. What is the best vacation you have ever had?	4. How often have you gone to that place?	5. What is the best food you have ever eaten?	6. How many times have you eaten it?	7. What is the best music you have ever heard?	8. How often have you listened to it?
1								
2								
3								
4								
5								

Now work in groups of four to compile the results of your surveys. For example, record how many people chose the same movie, etc. Present your results to the class.

Reading

Read the article and answer the questions that follow.

ASHRITA FURMAN

Ashrita Furman (Keith Furman) was born in Brooklyn, New York, in 1954, the same year the *Guinness Book of Records* was created. Ashrita has <u>captured</u> the public's imagination by breaking Guinness world records under <u>outrageous</u> conditions and in the most exotic places. He currently holds more than 175 Guinness records, including the official record for holding the most records! Since setting his first record of 27,000 jumping jacks in 1979, Ashrita has broken more than 300 records overall.

Ashrita has broken a Guinness record on every continent, including hula hooping for the fastest mile at Ayers Rock (Uluru) in the Australian bush and completing the fastest mile on a pogo stick in Antarctica. Ashrita has also set records at many famous landmarks around the world, including standing on a <u>Swiss ball</u> for the longest time at Stonehenge in England, balancing a pool cue while walking the longest distance at the pyramids in Egypt, skipping rope the most times in a minute while jumping on a pogo stick at Angkor Wat in Cambodia, and bouncing the fastest mile on a kangaroo ball along the Great Wall of China.

Ashrita has been practising <u>meditation</u> for more than 30 years and sees his records as a way to demonstrate the benefits of this ancient Eastern art. The name "Ashrita" is Sanskrit, meaning "protected by God." It was given to him by his meditation teacher, Sri Chinmoy, whom Ashrita credits for his remarkable <u>endurance</u> and strength. "I am not a natural athlete, but my teacher has shown me that if one can be in touch with one's inner spirit, anything is possible."

Ashrita has walked 80 miles with a milk bottle balanced on his head, has performed 9,628 sit-ups (crunches) in an hour, has balanced a 93-pound stack of milk crates on his chin, and has balanced 700 eggs on end <u>simultaneously</u>. However, Ashrita's greatest challenge was probably his feat of performing forward rolls for the entire 12-mile length of Paul Revere's ride in Massachusetts. The unofficial rule is that the rolls have to be continuous, but you are allowed to stop to throw up!

Ashrita loves a challenge. Almost every week, he hears of someone somewhere in the world who has broken one of his records. His only reaction is to work harder in order to retake the record. Ashrita currently lives in New York and manages a health food store there.

Source: Ashrita Furman's website http://www.ashrita.com

COMPREHENSION

Use the correct verb tense to answer the following questions. Write complete sentences.

1. How many records has Ashrita Furman broken?

2. How many continents has he gone to in order to break his records?

_____

3. What record has he broken in the following locations?

- Australia
- Antarctica
- England
- Cambodia

_____

_____

_____

4. What has Ashrita been practising for more than 30 years?

_____

5. What has Ashrita learned from his spiritual teacher?

_____

6. Explain the records Ashrita has broken using the following feats:

- milk bottle balancing
- sit-ups
- milk crate balancing
- egg balancing

_____

_____

_____

_____

7. What is Ashrita's everyday job?

_____

8. What does Ashrita do when he hears someone else has broken one of his old records?

_____

ANALYZING THE READING PASSAGE

Look through the reading a second time. Underline all the verbs in the present perfect tense with a single line, and all the verbs in the present perfect progressive with a double line.

Listening

🔊 *Track 8*

GUINNESS BOOK OF WORLD RECORDS

Listen to the audio clip once. Write **T** for the statements below that are true and **F** for the statements that are false. Then correct the false statements.

1. _____ Both guests on the program have been in the *Guinness Book* more than once.

2. _____ The *Guinness Book of Records* was first published in August 1954.

3. _____ The main offices of Guinness World Records are in Canada.

4. _____ A new edition of the *Guinness Book* is published every year.

5. _____ Other people have already broken Larry Olmsted's records.

6. _____ All new records are published in the annual edition of the *Guinness Book*.

7. _____ The easiest way to get into the *Guinness Book* is to be a top athlete in the world at a particular sport.

8. _____ Ashrita believes God tells him to break records.

9. _____ In 1981 Ashrita clapped his hands for 50 days.

10. _____ Ashrita becomes sad when other people break his records, but he tries hard to retake the records.

COMPREHENSION

Listen to the program again and answer the following questions. Write complete sentences.

1. How many copies of the Guinness book have been sold so far?

_____

2. In how many languages has the book been published?

_____

3. Which of these people would *not* appear in the book? Choose one.

- the person who has missed the fewest days of school
- the person who has gotten the most tattoos
- the person who has played the longest game of cards
- the person who has been married more times than anyone else

_____

4. What is the subject of the book Larry Olmsted has written?

_____

5. How many record categories does Guinness have? How many are published every year?

_____

_____

6. Other people have tried to publish records books. Most of them
   a) have survived.
   b) have not survived.

7. How many records has Ashrita Furman set or broken so far?

_____

8. What advice does Ashrita give other people who are interested in setting or breaking records?

_____

Writing

Choose one of the topics below. Write a short composition (maximum 250 words) about the topic.

- What accomplishments have you had in your life so far?
- What technological advances have you witnessed since you were born?

CHAPTER REVIEW

Summary

Use the present perfect in the following situations:

- For actions that took place in the past, at an uncertain or unspecified time:

   Have you ever been to Rome?

   No, I haven't, but I have been to Venice. I went there last year.

- For actions that started in the past and that are still continuing.

   - We often use *for* or *since* with these sentences:

      How long have you been a vegetarian?

      I've been a vegetarian since 2002. I gave up meat when I was 16.

- For repeated past actions:

   I've seen that movie three times already!

   I've had pizza for dinner four times this week.

EXERCISE 1

Fill in the blanks with the simple past or the present perfect of the verb in parentheses.

1. _____ (Marie, ever, write) a poem?

2. When _____ (he, go) there? He _____ (go) there last month.

3. Yesterday I _____ (watch) a fantastic movie.

4. They _____ (not, come) to the party last night because they _____ (be) sick.

5. James _____ (graduate) from college last year. He _____ (work) for this company since September.

EXERCISE 2

1. There are five verb tense errors in the following passage. Find and correct them.

   Frank and I are friends for a long time. We met while we were in high school. We have played hockey on the same team back then. Unfortunately, I didn't played hockey since that time, but Frank has continued to play. His current team is quite good and I watched them play many times. Have you played a team sport in high school?

2. There are six errors in the following passage. They may include problems with the verb tense, the use of *for* and *since*, the order of adverbs, irregular verbs, or subject / verb agreement. Find and correct them.

   Michelle always dreamed of becoming a computer programmer. She wants to design gaming software. She have been playing computer games since she has been a little girl. She never worked for a computer company, but she taught herself a lot. She has been studying at the college since two years and next semester she'll do her internship at a software design company. She has heard really good things about the company and is looking forward to working there.

EXERCISE 3

Change each of the following positive sentences into the negative.

She has had lots of training in her job. → She hasn't had much training in her job.

They have travelled to many places. → They haven't travelled to many places.

1. You have eaten too many candies.

2. I have written many pages.

   _____

3. She has slept for a long time.

   _____

4. It has rained since we got here.

   _____

5. We have already eaten our snacks.

   _____

EXERCISE 4

Change each of the following sentences into a yes / no question.

We have had lunch. → Have you had lunch?

He has left. → Has he left?

1. I have eaten breakfast. _____?

2. She has slept. _____?

3. They have gone. _____?

4. The students have written their exams already. _____?

5. We have seen the movie. _____?

EXERCISE 5

Change each of the following sentences to a wh- (information) question. The information you want to ask about is **bolded** and underlined.

He has left **because he was tired**. → Why has he left?

They have received this document **by email**. → How have they received this document?

1. He has travelled to **Machu Picchu**.

   _____?

2. They have eaten **veggie burgers**.

   _____?

3. We have been **to the concert**.

   _____?

4. The children have tried **the new ice-cream flavour**.

_____?

5. The athletes have run **for five hours**.

_____?

EXERCISE 6

Fill in the blanks with the present perfect progressive form of the verbs in parentheses.

1. I _____ (cook) dinner for three hours and you haven't even helped me peel the potatoes!

2. She _____ (wait) for that letter for two weeks now. She is getting anxious.

3. The children _____ (help) their mother bake cookies. There is flour and sugar all over the kitchen.

4. I'm so sorry I'm late. _____ (you, sit) here for a long time?

5. They cancelled the soccer game because it _____ (rain) since Monday.

EXERCISE 7

Circle the letter of the correct answer.

1. He _____ of becoming a police officer.
   a) have always been dreaming
   b) has dreamed always
   c) has always dreamed

2. They _____ last May.
   a) have known each other since
   b) have known each other for
   c) have been knowing each other since

3. I _____ 45 minutes to see the teacher.
   a) waited since
   b) have been waiting for
   c) have been waiting since

4. _____ a snake?
   a) Have you eaten ever
   b) Have you never eaten
   c) Have you ever eaten

5. How many times _____ this movie?
   a) has she been seeing
   b) has she seen
   c) she has seen

Modals

PART 2

7 COMBINING CLAUSES

8 PRESENT PERFECT

9 MODALS

10 TYPES OF QUESTIONS AND SHORT ANSWERS

11 PREPOSITIONS AND PHRASAL VERBS

12 PAST PERFECT AND CONDITIONALS

OVERVIEW

Modals are auxiliary verbs. We use them to indicate another aspect of the main verb—for example, ability, necessity, permission, advice. Modals do not change form (we do not add -*s* to a third-person modal). They are followed by the base form of the verb. Sometimes, we use a phrase in place of a modal. These modal phrases include *ought to*, *be able to*, and *have to*. They are often more common in spoken English.

- Some modals (*can*, *could*, *be able to*) are used to show ability:

  She **can** play the violin beautifully.

  I **could** speak much better Spanish when I was younger.

  Sadly, **I'm not able to** go to their wedding.

- Some modals (*must*, *must not*, *have to*) are used to show necessity or obligation:

  You **must** pay your tuition fees before the end of the month.

  You **mustn't** share this information with anyone; it's a secret.

  We **have to** get up early to go to the airport.

- Some modals (*should*, *ought to*, *could*, *had better*) are used to give advice or make suggestions:

  You **should** thank them for their generous gift.

  You **ought to** return the rental car before you are charged for another day.

  You **could** ask for a few more shifts at work.

  You**'d better** call him and apologize right away.

- Some modals (*can*, *may*, *could*, *would*) are used to make polite requests or ask permission:

  Can I open the window?

  May I borrow your pen?

  Could I please come in?

  Would you get me a glass of water?

- Some modals (*must*, *may*, *might*, *could*) are used to show present or future possibility:

  We **may** be a little late, so go ahead and eat without us.

  Look at those clouds; it **might** rain tonight.

  We **could** win the Championship if we play well in the last few games.

Warm-up

Work in pairs. Look at the sentences below. What does the modal in each sentence show? Discuss your choice, and then circle the correct answer.

1. Could you open the window, please?

   ability / necessity / advice / request / possibility

2. You have to sign this document.

   ability / necessity / advice / request / possibility

3. You should see a doctor about that cough.

   ability / necessity / advice / request / possibility

4. All passengers must show their passports at the border.

   ability / necessity / advice / request / possibility

5. It may be possible to get an extension; ask your professor.

   ability / necessity / advice / request / possibility

6. May I ask a question?

   ability / necessity / advice / request / possibility

7. They can dance very well; they have taken lessons.

   ability / necessity / advice / request / possibility

8. We ought to head out. We need to get to the station by eleven o'clock.

   ability / necessity / advice / request / possibility

MODALS EXPRESSING ABILITY

Warm-up

Complete the following sentences. Two of your sentences should be true; the third should be false.

- I can _____ .

- I am able to _____ .

- When I was a child, I could _____ .

Now work in groups of three. Share your sentences with your group. Don't say which are true and which is false. Your group members should ask questions to find out which sentence is not true.

Formation

Modal	Sentence Type	Example Sentences (Present and Past)
can be able to	positive statement	I **can** ride a horse. I **could** dance when I was a child. I **am able to** meet you today. I **was able to** understand the article.
	negative statement	I **can't** ride a horse. I **couldn't** dance when I was a child. I **am not able to** meet you today. I **was not able to** understand the article.
	question	**Can** you ride a horse? **Could** you ride a horse when you were a child? **Are** you **able to** meet me today? **Are** you **able to** understand the article?

EXERCISE 1

Travis is talking to his girlfriend, Francine. Fill in each blank with the correct word: *can, can't, could,* or *couldn't.*

Travis: When I was a kid, I was a genius. You won't believe the things I _____ do.

Francine: Oh? Like what?

Travis: My dad was in the army, and we travelled a lot. I _____ speak six languages before I was 10. I _____ speak English, French, Russian, Arabic,

Chinese, Spanish, and Portuguese. The only one I _____ learn was Korean; it was too difficult!

Francine: _____ you still speak all those languages?

Travis: No, I _____. I've forgotten most of them. You know what else I _____ do? I _____ fix things. When our television broke, no one else _____ figure out what to do, but I repaired it. I was only seven.

Francine: I don't believe you! You _____ fix my DVD player!

Travis: No, you're right. I've forgotten those skills.

Francine: What else _____ you do?

Travis: Oh, I _____ ride horses, I _____ play three musical instruments, and I _____ even do the difficult crossword in the newspaper.

Francine: How about now? _____ you cook dinner? Vacuum the floor? Do the laundry? Take the dog for a walk? I bet you _____!

Travis: Uh . . . maybe. But I _____ right now. I have to visit my mother. See you later!

EXERCISE 2

Read the following passage about college valedictorian Daniel Lafortune. Then write six sentences about Daniel. Three should be about things he could (was able to) do in the past; the other three should be about things he can (is able to) do now.

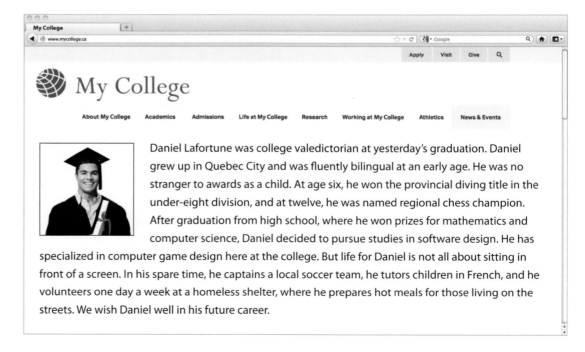

My College

Daniel Lafortune was college valedictorian at yesterday's graduation. Daniel grew up in Quebec City and was fluently bilingual at an early age. He was no stranger to awards as a child. At age six, he won the provincial diving title in the under-eight division, and at twelve, he was named regional chess champion. After graduation from high school, where he won prizes for mathematics and computer science, Daniel decided to pursue studies in software design. He has specialized in computer game design here at the college. But life for Daniel is not all about sitting in front of a screen. In his spare time, he captains a local soccer team, he tutors children in French, and he volunteers one day a week at a homeless shelter, where he prepares hot meals for those living on the streets. We wish Daniel well in his future career.

1. _____
2. _____
3. _____
4. _____
5. _____
6. _____

COMMUNICATIVE ACTIVITY 1

Unique Talents

Think of an activity that you can do but that you think none of your classmates can do. Write it here:

I can _____ .

Walk around the room asking your classmates, "I can _____. Can you?"

Write down the names of all your classmates who can also do the skill you chose. The winner is the student with the fewest names.

MODALS EXPRESSING NECESSITY OR OBLIGATION

Warm-up

Work with a partner. Think about the place where you are living right now: college residence, apartment, your parents' home, or somewhere else. What are some things you must (have to) do? What are some things you must not do? What are some things you don't have to do? Some ideas are given to you.

"I don't have to" does not have the same meaning as "I must not." We use "I must not" when something is forbidden. "I don't have to" has the same meaning as "I don't need to" (it isn't necessary).

I must / I have to . . .	I must not . . .	I don't have to . . .
keep my room clean.	smoke indoors.	pay for the Internet.

Formation

Modal	Use	Sentence Type	Example Sentences (Present and Past)
must have to	expressing necessity	positive statement	I **must** work late tonight. I **have to** study for my exams. (There is no past tense of *must*.) I **had to** go to the hospital last week.
		question	**Must** you work so late? Do you **have to** study for your exams? (There is no past tense of *must*.) Did you **have to** study for your exams?
must not, mustn't	expressing that something is forbidden	negative statement	You **must not** smoke in the cafeteria. We **mustn't** work together on this assignment.
don't have to	expressing that something is not necessary	negative statement	You **don't have to** come with me; I can go alone. It's okay; you **don't have to** lend me any money.

EXERCISE 3

Look at the following signs. Next to each one, write its meaning.
Use "We must / We have to . . ." or "We must not . . ."

We must stop. / We have to stop.

1. _____

2. _____

3. _____

4. _____

5. _____

EXERCISE 4

Choose between *mustn't* and *don't have to / doesn't have to* in the following sentences. (Circle) the correct answer.

1. You (**must not / don't have to**) wear business clothes to work. You can wear jeans if you want to.

2. You (**must not / don't have to**) park here. This space is for disabled drivers.

3. The children (**must not / don't have to**) go outside without telling their parents.

4. We (**must not / don't have to**) pay in cash; we can use a credit card.

5. She (**must not / doesn't have to**) work this weekend, so we can go out.

COMMUNICATIVE ACTIVITY 2

In The Know

Next term, your school will welcome a new group of students. They will not know any of the rules, or what they have to do. Work in small groups. Make a list of useful information to help these new students in their first term.

Think about things the new students must do, things they must not do, and things they don't have to do.

MODALS FOR GIVING ADVICE AND MAKING SUGGESTIONS

Warm-up

As a class, brainstorm what you consider to be junk food. Then, give advice and make suggestions using modals as in the example below:

Too much candy can harm our teeth. We should eat less. We should brush our teeth after eating sweets.

French fries have lots of calories. We ought to reduce the number of fries we eat.

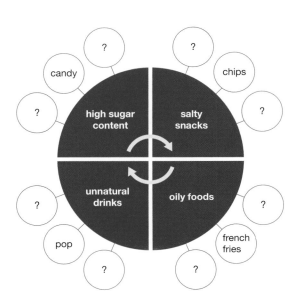

Formation

Modal	Use	Sentence Type	Example Sentences
should ought to could had better	making a suggestion / giving advice	positive statement	You **should** pay your utilities bill before your electricity is cut off. You **ought to** rest for a while. You **could** pay your fees in advance to avoid interest charges. **You'd better*** renew your passport if you're planning to travel next summer.
		negative statement	You **shouldn't** forget to pay your utilities bills, or your electricity will be cut off. You **ought not** hesitate **to** rest for a while. (There is no negative for *could*.) **You'd better not*** forget to renew your passport if you're planning to travel next summer.
		question	**Should** you pay your utilities bill? **Ought** you **to** rest for a while? **Could** you pay your fees in advance to avoid interest charges? **Hadn't** you **better** renew your passport if you're planning to travel next summer? **Why don't** you buy a car, so you won't need to take the bus?

Note that "You had (You'd) better . . ." is quite strong and often sounds harsh (for example, like a parent speaking to a child or a boss speaking to an employee).

EXERCISE 5

Give advice to the following people using one of the modals in the chart above.

I want to save money to travel.

You could find a part-time job.

1. I want to make more friends.

   You _____

2. I want to be more confident.

   You _____

3. I want to get in better shape.

   You _____

4. I want to find a boyfriend / girlfriend.

   You _____

5. I want to give up smoking.

You _____

EXPRESSING REGRET: MODALS IN THE PAST

We use *I should (not) have* + past participle for things that we now regret doing or regret not doing. These sentences indicate actions that were carried out for no good reason or past ability that was not acted upon.

I forgot my father's birthday. I should have remembered!

Wendy looks terrible. She shouldn't have coloured her hair.

Harry is upset. We should have invited him to our party.

EXERCISE 6

What regrets do the following people have? Complete the sentences with *should have (should not have)* + past participle.

1. Denise's car was towed away because she parked in a no-parking zone.

   She _____

2. The Walkers' house was broken into while they were on vacation.

   They _____

3. I owe over $25,000 on my credit card!

   You _____

4. Crazy Crafts went out of business because it didn't make a profit for three years.

   The owners _____

5. The actress is suing the newspaper because it printed an untrue story about her.

   The newspaper editor _____

 # COMMUNICATIVE ACTIVITY 3

I Need Advice!

Divide into two groups.

Group A: You are all at a party with people of all ages and backgrounds. You are hoping to get some advice for different problems that you have. Your teacher will give you each a card with a problem on it. Walk around the room talking to the other guests. Ask several of them for a solution to your problem. Then, choose the best one.

Group B: You are also guests at the party. Give your best advice to each person with a problem.

When you have finished, change roles.

MODALS FOR MAKING POLITE REQUESTS AND ASKING PERMISSION

Warm-up

Work in pairs. Look at the following situations. How many ways can you think of to ask for what you want?

- You go to your professor's office to ask for more time to finish your assignment.
- You are at a very formal dinner, and you would like a glass of water.
- You really need to borrow money from a wealthy uncle that you don't know very well.

With a partner, discuss the differences in level of formality between the various sentences you have come up with.

Formation

Modal	Use	Example Sentences
can	making requests (informal to formal)	**Can** you open the door? **Can** you let me in early?
would		**Would** you open the door? **Would** you let me in early?
could		**Could** you open the door? **Could** you let me in early?
can	asking permission (informal to formal)	**Can** I hand in my paper tomorrow? **Can** I borrow your car?
may		**May** I hand in my paper tomorrow? **May** I borrow your car?

In English, the word *please* is often included in requests and permissions to make them more polite:

Can you open the window, please?　　　　May I please leave class early today?

Can you please open the window?

EXERCISE 7

Change each of the following imperatives to a polite request.

1. Check your mailbox.

   _____

2. Leave the keys at the front desk.

   _____

3. Return the hangers to the dry cleaners.

   _____

4. Turn up the heat in the sauna.

   _____

5. Answer the door.

   _____

EXERCISE 8

Imagine you are in these situations. What are you going to say?

1. Ask your friend's parents for permission to use their bathroom.

   _____

2. Ask a hotel concierge to book a taxi for you.

   _____

3. Ask a classmate to drive you to a school event.

   _____

4. Ask to try on a piece of clothing in a department store.

   _____

5. Ask your boss for permission to take Friday off.

   _____

MODALS FOR SHOWING PRESENT AND FUTURE POSSIBILITY

Warm-up

Work with a partner. If you see these symbols on your local weather report, what kind of weather might you have? Use the following:

It might be _____.

We might have _____.

We might have thundershowers tomorrow.

Formation

PRESENT POSSIBILITY

Modal	Use	Example Sentences
must	to show that you think something is definitely true	Larry has worked for 16 hours straight. He **must** be exhausted. Zahra is taking her driving test tomorrow. She **must** be nervous.
might may could	to show that you think something is possible	Look at that guy in the limo. He **might** be a movie star. We're having freezing rain. My classes **may** be cancelled. I don't know what I'm eating. It **could** be tofu.
can't	to show that you think something is not possible	Someone is at the door. It **can't** be John; he's in Mexico. This website says the population of Canada is 50 million. That **can't** be true!

FUTURE POSSIBILITY

Modal or Other Verb	Use	Example Sentences
will / going to	to show that you think something will definitely happen	I'm sure **we'll** have a lot of snow this winter. It's definitely **going to** rain tonight.
might may could	to show that you think something will possibly happen	I ordered some books online. They **might** arrive tomorrow. We **may** be a little late, so don't worry. We **could** have a thunderstorm; it feels humid.
might not may not	to show that you think something will *possibly not* happen	Don't worry. He **might not** be too angry. We **may not** go on vacation this year; we want to save our money. She **may not** renew her gym membership; she likes the gym on campus.
will not (won't)	to show that you think something will *definitely not* happen	Ten years from now, we **won't** have any more textbooks. Goodbye! I **won't** be late, I promise. Cancer and AIDS **won't** exist in the future.

EXERCISE 9

Circle the correct modal to complete the following sentences.

1. You haven't eaten anything today. You (must / might / can't) be starving.

2. The goalie let in eight goals in tonight's game. He (must / might / can't) be embarrassed.

3. I don't understand modern art. This (must / could / can't) be a horse, or it (must / may / can't) be a man with a large nose.

4. That guy over there looks like Pierre, but it (must / might / can't) be him. Pierre moved to Edmonton last summer.

5. Why aren't you wearing a scarf or mitts? You (must / may / can't) be freezing!

6. No one goes to the new Italian restaurant. It (must / might / can't) be very good.

7. I don't know why Carol is absent today. She (must / might / can't) be sick.

8. Li said she bought a brand-new laptop for $300, but that (must / might / can't) be true.

EXERCISE 10

Look at the following chart for the international weather channel's weekend travel report. Predict the weather in your own words using modals. Look at the example to help you.

Location	Saturday's Forecast	Weather Predictions
Edmonton, Alberta, Canada	15 degrees Celsius, sunshine, partly cloudy, 20% chance of rain	The temperature of Edmonton, Alberta, could be as high as 15 degrees Celsius for this Saturday. There will be sunshine but there will be some cloud too. There might be some rain, but it's not very likely.
Halifax, Nova Scotia, Canada	5 degrees Celsius, wind gusts up to 70 km/h	
Havana, Cuba	Tropical storm likely escalating to a category 1 hurricane. Wind and heavy downpours on the way—take all precautions.	
Beijing, China	High of 27 degrees Celsius. Sunshine and no rain in the forecast for the next 24 hours.	
Rio de Janeiro, Brazil	32 degrees Celsius—possibility of heavy rains up to 25 mm	
Yellowknife, Northwest Territories, Canada	15 cm of snow on the way, temperature dropping to −20 by late tonight. Wind chill factor of −35.	

❖ COMMUNICATIVE ACTIVITY 4

Where Could She Be?

Read the following news bulletin.

> **Breaking News //** Police are searching for meteorology professor Dr. Elizabeth Mason, 38, who disappeared from her home sometime late last week. Dr. Mason has not been seen since last Thursday, when she taught a class in climate change. Her family, friends, and colleagues have no idea where she might be. At the moment, foul play is not suspected.

Where is Dr. Mason? Your teacher will give you cards with information the police collected. Read each card in the correct order, and try to solve this mystery.

BRINGING IT ALL TOGETHER

COMMUNICATIVE ACTIVITY 5

Travel Advice

Work in groups of four. Choose one of the following destinations:

Petra, Jordan   Venice, Italy   Beijing, China   Patagonia, Argentina

Use your smartphone, tablet, or laptop to do some basic research. Fill in the following chart with important information that a visitor to your chosen place needs to know. Then, share your advice and recommendations with the class.

Destination: _____

Question	Recommendations
What can I see and do there? What are the top two or three sights?	
What will the weather be like?	
What should I pack?	
Do I have to get a visa, or any vaccinations?	
Are there any cultural taboos? (In other words, is there anything I must not say or do there?)	
Any other important information?	

Reading

Read the passage and answer the questions that follow.

ALIENS

How should you greet an <u>alien</u> if you meet one? What should you say? Should you be friendly or <u>cautious</u>? Can aliens even speak English?

These questions, of course, have been asked many times. Imaginative television producers who know that we are curious have created television programs with alien characters.

Of all the famous science-fiction (or sci-fi) TV aliens, we could say that Mr. Spock from the 1960s series *Star Trek* would likely make the top of the list as the most famous. You might know Spock for being completely logical and emotionless. His famous eyebrows and pointy ears have been a popular Halloween costume for decades, and will be for many more years. Many other alien characters, who could be considered much more lively than Spock, have been featured on situation comedy shows (<u>sitcoms</u>). The very first one that I remember is Uncle Martin from *My Favorite Martian*. I watched the <u>reruns</u> growing up. As a very young child, I wanted to believe that Uncle Martin—an anthropologist from Mars who crashed his spaceship on Earth—might be real. He seemed smart and wise. I wanted to believe Martians did exist and that I might meet one, one day.

At some point I had to accept that Martians may not exist and if they do, they certainly don't have antennas coming out of their heads, but then, in the 1970s, came *Mork and Mindy*. Mork, an alien, was assigned to experience the planet Earth and report back to his planet, Ork. Many things on our planet that we take for granted, Mork would see as new and different.

Then came *Alf* in the 1980s. This time a furry puppet character played the alien and he was quite likeable. His existence had to be a secret with the family that had found him because it would be a disaster if the world found out such a great secret.

Probably the funniest alien sitcom that viewers might remember featured the characters in the 1990s show *3rd Rock from the Sun*. These four characters were on a mission to find out about human beings and human behaviour, but it was their ignorance of our ways and traditions that made the show a comedy hit.

Where do we go from here? Can all these imagined visits from aliens actually prepare us for the real, eventful day of meeting extraterrestrials? Of course, many people say aliens can't possibly exist; they must exist only in our imaginations. Other people are not so sure. . . . One thing is for certain, though. If and when we do meet, we will sure hope that they have a sense of humour.

COMPREHENSION

Answer the following questions. Use complete sentences.

1. Which questions about aliens have people asked many times?

2. If you want to dress up as a TV alien for Halloween, which character could you choose?

_____

3. What should you do if you want to look like Mr. Spock?

_____

4. Why couldn't Alf's family tell anyone that he existed?

_____

DISCUSSION

Work in groups of three or four. Discuss the following:

1. Most people believe that aliens must be real. True or false? Give your reasons.

2. Do you think we might meet aliens one day in the future? Explain.

3. Do you like any sci-fi television shows? Why? What attracted you to these shows? If you don't like sci-fi shows, be prepared to tell the group why not.

Listening

◀)) *Track 9*

COUNSELLING SESSION

Listen to the audio. You will hear a conversation between a counsellor, Dr. James Sebastian, and his patient, Davood Taylor.

Listen to the conversation again. Every time you hear a modal, place a check mark (✓) in the appropriate box beside it in the "Heard" column of the chart. When you are finished, listen again to make sure you have the correct number of checks. If you didn't hear a specific modal, put an X.

Note: *should've = should have*; *could've = could have*

Modal	Heard	Negative Modal	Heard	Past Modal	Heard	Negative Past Modal	Heard
can		can't					
could		couldn't					
should		shouldn't		should have		shouldn't have	
have to		don't have to		had to		didn't have to	
ought to		ought not to					
must		mustn't					
will		will not					

COMPREHENSION

Listen again to Dr. Sebastian's advice. What should Davood do? What should he not do? Write five sentences in your own words.

_____

_____

_____

_____

_____

_____

_____

_____

_____

Writing

Imagine you can travel back in time. Think about a character in history that you would like to meet. What questions would you like to ask him or her? What would you like to know about his or her time in history? Write the script for a short interview (200 words) listing all the questions you have and giving possible answers.

CHAPTER REVIEW

Summary

- We use modals in the following situations:
  - to talk about ability in the present and the past
  - to talk about things that are necessary or things that are forbidden
  - to give advice and make suggestions
  - to make requests and ask permission
  - to talk about present or future possibility

- Modals don't change form (they don't add -s for third-person subjects). They are followed by the base form of the verb.
- There are some phrases that have the same use as modal verbs (for example, *ought to*, *be able to*, and *have to*). These do change form.

EXERCISE 1

Circle the best choice of modal. Then write it in the blank and read the sentence to yourself to check it.

1. We _____ (must not / don't have to) hand in our report on Friday. We can wait until Monday.

2. I _____ (should / should have) sent the letter on Friday.

3. I don't know what language those people are speaking. It _____ (must / might) be Swedish.

4. We _____ (ought to / should to) eat more healthy food.

5. _____ (May / Can) you text me from the bus, so I know you're on your way?

6. You _____ (had better / had better to) hurry up, or you'll be late.

7. That girl has never heard of Sidney Crosby! She _____ (could / can't) be Canadian.

8. _____ (Can I / Can I to) borrow your headphones to listen to this song?

EXERCISE 2

Read Person B's answers in the following. What do you think Person A's question might be? Use your imagination; there is more than one correct answer. Look at the example to help you.

Person A: <u>Can you play an instrument?</u>

Person B: I could play the guitar when I was a student, but now I can't play anything.

1. Person A: _____?

   Person B: The weather report says it might rain.

2. Person A: _____?

   Person B: I think you should change your hairstyle.

3. Person A: _____?

   Person B: Sure. It is hot in here, isn't it?

4. Person A: _____?

   Person B: No, that can't be true. I don't believe it.

5. Person A: _____?

   Person B: Yes, of course. Come on in!

6. Person A: _____?

   Person B: You don't have to, but you can if you want to.

EXERCISE 3

Read the following sentences about Magic Majid. Each sentence contains *at least* one error. Find the errors and correct them.

1. As a boy, Majid loved magic. He could to do card tricks and make coins disappear.

2. Everyone always applauded him and said, "You ought become a professional magician!"

3. He wanted to become a magician, but his parents said, "You should paying more attention to your school work."

4. They told him, "You don't have to waste time on this silly magic. You better go to university and study math and science."

5. Majid went to university, but he was unhappy. He can't understand why his parents thought science was so important.

6. He begged them, "Can I please dropping these courses?"

7. But one day, something magical happened. Majid heard his physics professor talking about quantum physics. He can't believe his ears! This was fascinating!

8. "I should have been listen to my parents," thought Majid. "They can't be right. Maybe science is interesting after all."

9. Majid grew to love science, and he graduated at the top of his class. "I not give up magic," he said. "There is magic in science."

10. Today Majid is a well-known science professor. He could still doing magic tricks, but he only does them for his wife and children.

Types of Questions and Short Answers

PART 2

7 COMBINING CLAUSES

8 PRESENT PERFECT

9 MODALS

10 TYPES OF QUESTIONS AND SHORT ANSWERS

11 PREPOSITIONS AND PHRASAL VERBS

12 PAST PERFECT AND CONDITIONALS

OVERVIEW

In this chapter we will explore different types of questions: yes / no, wh- (information) questions, and tag questions. We will take a short look at negative questions along the way.

• Yes / no questions are very simple. Short answers to yes / no questions are used primarily in spoken English:

Are you a student? Yes, I am.   Can you play the guitar? No, I can't.

Did you enjoy the movie? Yes, I did.

• Information questions begin with the words *who*, *what*, *where*, *when*, *why*, and *how*. We use them when we need a specific piece of information:

Who is coming to your party?   How many courses are you taking?

Where were you born?   Why did you tell everyone my secret?

• Tag questions appear at the end of a sentence and may be either positive or negative. They are primarily used in spoken English when the speaker is looking for confirmation about an idea or opinion:

It's cold in here, isn't it?   We had a great vacation, didn't we?

You're Ed's brother, aren't you?

YES / NO (INTERROGATIVE) QUESTIONS

Warm-up

Work with a partner. Look at the chart below. How do you think your partner will answer these questions? Guess your partner's answers with a check mark (✓) each time. Next, interview your partner using the situation description. Were your guesses correct?

Key:

1 – No, definitely not!
2 – I don't think so.
3 – Perhaps; I'm not sure.
4 – I think so.
5 – Yes, definitely.

	Situation	Response				
		1	2	3	4	5
A	You have the chance to volunteer for six months in a very poor country. It will be a difficult life with hard work and the possibility of illness. Will you go?					
B	You are offered a well-paying job as a telemarketer. However, the job requires you to raise money for a political cause you do not believe in. Do you accept?					
C	You are taking a course you really love, and you have two years left. Your fiancé(e) has been offered a job in another province. Do you quit your course and go with him or her?					

Formation

With the verb *be*, you can create a yes / no question in the simple present and simple past tenses by switching the placement of the subject and verb.

He is happy. → Is he happy?

There were cars on the street. → Were there cars on the street?

With other verbs in past and present tense, the auxiliary *do* must be added to create a yes / no question. The main verb is then used in its base form.

She runs a marathon each year. → Does she run a marathon each year?

He went to Spain last year. → Did he go to Spain last year?

When there is a modal, you can switch the placement of the subject and the modal in the same way that you do with the verb *be*.

He can play the piano. → Can he play the piano?

We should leave soon. → Should we leave soon?

A modal is an auxiliary verb and follows the same rules as the other auxiliary verbs: *do*, *be*, and *have*.

EXERCISE 1

Change the following statements into yes / no questions. Remember to add the question mark.

That apartment has a view of the river. → Does that apartment have a view of the river?

1. We are preparing for the final exam.

   _____

2. They have signed the lease for six months.

   _____

3. The floors in the apartment were wet.

   _____

4. We should look at the other apartment.

   _____

5. She was writing an email when the accident happened.

   _____

6. The soup is hot.

   _____

SHORT ANSWERS TO YES / NO QUESTIONS

When answering a yes / no question in spoken English, it is more polite to answer with more than just a yes or a no. To form a polite short answer, follow the pattern in the chart below.

Tense	Question	Positive Response	Negative Response
simple present	Is she happy with her course? Does he want the job? Should we travel to Spain?	Yes, she is. Yes, he does. Yes, you should.	No, she isn't. No, he doesn't. No, you shouldn't.
present progressive	Is it snowing?	Yes, it is.	No, it isn't.

Continued

Tense	Question	Positive Response	Negative Response
simple past	Were you sick yesterday? Did you go to the concert? Could you ride a horse as a child?	Yes, I was. Yes, I did. Yes, I could.	No, I wasn't. No, I didn't. No, I couldn't.
future with *will*	Will they pay the bill?	Yes, they will.	No, they won't.
future with *be going to*	Are they going to share a taxi?	Yes, they are.	No, they're not.
past progressive	Were you sleeping?	Yes, I was.	No, I wasn't.
present perfect	Have you finished your lunch?	Yes, I have.	No, I haven't.
present perfect progressive	Have you been studying for the test?	Yes, I have.	No, I haven't.

EXERCISE 2

Respond to the following questions with short answers.

Are you from New Brunswick? Yes, I am. / No, I'm not.

1. Are the Johnstons your friends?   Yes, _____ No, _____

2. Has your sister studied Spanish?   Yes, _____ No, _____

3. Should your son buy a car?   Yes, _____ No, _____

4. Can the mechanic fix your car?   Yes, _____ No, _____

5. Have you been waiting long?   Yes, _____ No, _____

6. Did they see the movie?   Yes, _____ No, _____

7. Will you sign the contract?   Yes, _____ No, _____

8. Does she swim well?   Yes, _____ No, _____

EXERCISE 3

Fill in the correct short answer to each question. Use the answers in the Choices column. Look at the example to help you.

Question	Correct Response	Choices
Are you comfortable?	Yes, I am.	No, she couldn't.
Could Ana help me?		No, he doesn't.
Will they come to the party?		Yes, they are.

Continued

Question	Correct Response	Choices
Does he drink beer?		No, I wouldn't.
Are the Shaws arriving by bus?		Yes, they have.
Would you like a coffee?		~~Yes, I am.~~
Have they flown before?		Yes, they were.
Were they singing well?		No, she hasn't.
Has she found her pen?		Yes, they will.

 # COMMUNICATIVE ACTIVITY 1

Landlords and Tenants Role-Play

Divide into two groups of 12.

Group A: You are landlords. You each have an apartment to rent, but you need to find the right tenant.

Group B: You are tenants. You are each looking for an apartment, but it has to meet your very specific needs.

Your teacher will give each member of your group a different a card that describes the character he or she will play. Read the information on your card, and by asking people in the other group questions, find the best match.

Here are some sample questions and answers that might be used:

Landlord: Have you ever been in jail?

Tenant: No, I haven't.

Tenant: Does your apartment have a big kitchen?

Landlord: Yes, it does.

NEGATIVE QUESTIONS

Formation

Most questions are asked using positive forms (Are you . . . ? Can you . . . ?). Sometimes, questions can use negative forms; we do this to get confirmation from the listener, often in a situation we are surprised about.

For example, you arrive at a classroom in time for a 9:00 AM class, but no one is there. A classmate arrives shortly after you. You might say,

Doesn't the class start at 9:00 AM?

You are expecting your classmate to confirm this and to give the answer, "Yes, it does."

Or, imagine your friend is looking for an apartment. He needs to call a rental agent. You think he has not done this, and you are surprised (and perhaps annoyed). You might say,

Haven't you called the rental agent yet?

You are expecting your friend to confirm this, and to say, "No, I haven't."

If, however, your friend *has* called the rental agent, he will give a positive response. This might be emphasized with an expression like *of course*, *certainly*, and *most definitely*:

Yes, of course I have called her.　　　　**I certainly have called her.**

To form a negative question, follow the chart below.

Tense	Statement	Negative Question
simple present	She is pretty.	Isn't she pretty?
present progressive	They are training for the race.	Aren't they training for the race?
simple past	He won a talent competition.	Didn't he win a talent competition?
future with *will*	He'll be disappointed with his results.	Won't he be disappointed with his results?
future with *be going to*	She's going to quit her job.	Isn't she going to quit her job?
past progressive	She was eating a banana.	Wasn't she eating a banana?
present perfect	They have sold their house.	Haven't they sold their house?
present perfect progressive	You've been learning to drive.	Haven't you been learning to drive?

EXERCISE 4

With a partner, create a negative question using the contraction of *not* for the sentence endings below. Each uses a phrase from the following list. Look at the example to help you.

Isn't she worried	Wasn't it scary	Wasn't it windy	Aren't you glad
Weren't you afraid	Weren't they proud	Wasn't she surprised	~~Isn't it wonderful~~

Isn't it wonderful that we have sunny weather for our picnic?

1. _____ your worries are over now?

2. _____ by her brother's unexpected news?

3. _____ of their sister?

4. _____ yesterday?

5. _____ about her marks?

6. _____ of an accident?

7. _____ watching that horror movie alone?

EXERCISE 5

With a partner, complete the following chart.

Statement: I think . . .	Negative Question: I ask . . .
You are glad the semester is over.	Aren't you glad the semester is over?
We were all cold in class this morning.	
He is worried about his taxes.	
She was anxious about her test results.	
It was hot in the library yesterday.	
There is a chill in the air today.	
They were surprised at the news.	
They were not prepared for the fire drill.	
There were a lot of hard questions.	

COMMUNICATIVE ACTIVITY 2

Assumptions

Part 1: Look at the following list of adjectives in the middle column. Put each word in the correct group. Add any others that you can think of. Look at the examples to help you.

Physical Feeling	Adjective	Emotional Feeling
	terrified	
	freezing	
	nervous	
	ashamed	
	amazed	
	upset	
	starving	
	furious	
	exhausted	
	depressed	
	thirsty	
	embarrassed	
	worried	
	frustrated	
	jealous	

Part 2: Your teacher will give you a pile of cards. Take turns to choose one. Select a person in your group, and make an assumption about how that person felt. The other person will respond to your assumption, using an adjective from the list above, or another expression.

Card: I heard you came home and found a rat in your kitchen. Weren't you scared?

Yes, I was. I was terrified.

No, not really. I'm not afraid of rats.

INFORMATION QUESTIONS

Warm-up

Work in groups of three or four. Discuss the answers to these questions with your group.

- You have won a round-trip plane ticket to anywhere in the world. Where are you going to go? Why have you chosen this destination?
- Your prize is for two people. Who might you invite to go with you?
- You have an added challenge: you are only allowed to take one carry-on piece of luggage. What can you pack in your carry-on bag?

Formation

Information questions are formed according to the following pattern.

Statement	Information Question
Fatima won the English prize.	**Who** won the English prize?
Our group project is about **climate change**.	**What** is your group project about?
I went to Portugal **last spring**.	**When** did you go to Portugal?
Ali lives **in an apartment downtown**.	**Where** does Ali live?
She works at night **because she has classes during the day**.	**Why** does she work at night?
Those gloves are **Claire's**.	**Whose** gloves are those?
I opened the parcel **with a knife**.	**How** did you open the parcel?
Dini has **five sisters**.	**How many** sisters does Dini have?
We've lived here **for 25 years**.	**How long** have you lived here?

EXERCISE 6

Change each of the following sentences to an information question. The information you want to ask about is **bolded** and underlined. Remember to add the question mark.

He should study for the exam **after the class.** → When should he study for the exam?

1. I went to **an exhibition of modern art** last night.

   _____

2. The art gallery was **downtown, near the station**.

   _____

3. I went to the art gallery **on the subway**.

   _____

4. I was late **because I fell asleep on the train and missed my stop**.

   _____

5. I arrived **five minutes before the gallery closed**.

   _____

6. There were **only three people** in the gallery.

   _____

7. **The gallery owner** introduced me to the artist.

   _____

8. After the gallery closed, I chatted with the artist **for two hours**.

   _____

9. We talked about **art, music, politics, and lots of other things**.

   _____

10. We're going **to a jazz festival** on Saturday afternoon!

   _____

EXERCISE 7

Read the paragraph below and then turn the page.

My sister bought a new television last week. **Several** models were on sale. **The 41-inch screen television** was still in the box from the factory. **The floor model** did not have the original packaging but **it** had an extended warranty. **Three warranty packages** were available at additional cost. **My father** lent my sister some money to buy the television. **A new television** is now in my sister's bedroom.

Write questions about the information in bold print in the paragraph. Use the question words *who*, *how many*, *what*, and *which*. Look at the example to help you.

<u>Who</u> bought a new television last week?

_____

_____

_____

_____

_____

_____

_____

COMMUNICATIVE ACTIVITY 3

Dream Lives

Imagine your dream identity. Are you a movie star, a soccer player, or the president of your home country? What is your name? Where do you live? What do you do? Write the information in the space provided in the chart below.

Now, work in groups of four. Tell your group your name and age.

You will have two dice. Take turns throwing the dice and asking / answering questions about your perfect identities. For example, if you throw a six, tell your group about your friends.

1	name and age	
2	place of residence	
3	job or other source of income	
4	daily routine	
5	family	
6	friends	
7	hobbies	
8	pets	
9	appearance, clothing, etc.	
10	transportation	
11	food	
12	personal goal	

TAG QUESTIONS

Warm-up

Imagine that you have just woken up from a long sleep and are a little confused. You have asked your roommate to help you confirm if you remember some things correctly. Complete these sentences with the correct information about yourself, then use a tag from the following list to complete each sentence. You will use each tag only once. Look at the example to help you. When you have finished, compare your answers with a partner.

~~isn't it~~	didn't I	can't I	aren't I	won't I	don't I

1. My name is **Lee, isn't it?**

2. I live in _____, _____?

3. I'm studying _____, _____?

4. I _____ on the weekend, _____?

5. I can _____, _____?

6. I will _____, _____?

Formation

By adding a tag question to the end of a sentence, the speaker wants to confirm an idea or thought or ask for information. Tag questions are primarily used in spoken, not written, English.

To form a tag question, use only the auxiliary verb from the main statement. If the main statement has only a main verb, use only the verb *do* in the tag. No other verbs are used. In writing, remember to use a comma (,) before the tag.

An affirmative (positive) statement requires a negative tag. A negative statement requires a positive tag. To form tag questions, follow the charts below.

POSITIVE STATEMENT + NEGATIVE TAG

Tense	Formation	Expected Response
simple present	You're in my class, **aren't you**? She speaks English well, **doesn't she**?	Yes, I am. Yes, she does.
present progressive	You're coming, **aren't you**?	Yes, I am.

Continued

Tense	Formation	Expected Response
simple past	She emailed you, **didn't she**?	Yes, she did.
future with *will*	She will graduate, **won't she**?	Yes, she will.
future with *be going to*	You're going to pay for the tickets, **aren't you**?	Yes, I am.
past progressive	You were fighting, **weren't you**?	Yes, we were.
present perfect	You've seen the movie, **haven't you**?	Yes, I have.
present perfect progressive	You've been smoking, **haven't you**?	Yes, I have.

NEGATIVE STATEMENT + POSITIVE TAG

Tense	Statement + Tag Question	Expected Response
simple present	They aren't rich, **are they**? They can't afford it, **can they**?	No, they're not. No, they can't.
present progressive	You're not crying, **are you**?	No, I'm not.
simple past	He didn't tell you the news, **did he**?	No, he didn't.
past progressive	You weren't listening, **were you**?	No, we weren't.
present perfect	You haven't read this book, **have you**?	No, I haven't.
present perfect progressive	You haven't been practising, **have you**?	No, I haven't.
future with *will*	She won't fail, **will she**?	No, she won't.
future with *be going to*	They are not going to complain, **are they**?	No, they're not.

If the main statement has only the main verb *be*, use the verb *be* in the tag.

EXERCISE 8

Complete the following tag questions with the appropriate tag.

Sarah is from New Brunswick, _____isn't she_____?

1. Cars pollute the environment, _____?

2. The books are very expensive, _____?

3. He hasn't called you, _____?

4. She went to class yesterday, _____?

5. They have travelled extensively, _____?

6. She should arrive soon, _____?

7. He can't fix the laptop, _____?

8. He goes to the gym every day, _____?

9. Jean had a bicycle, _____?

10. We could go to the movies, _____?

EXERCISE 9

Write tag questions in the chart provided. All of the questions should be different, and each should use a different tense. Use contractions wherever possible.

Pronoun	Positive Statement + Negative Tag	Negative Statement + Positive Tag
I	I was honest, wasn't I?	I wasn't honest, was I?
You (singular)		
He		
She		
It		
We		
You (plural)		
They		

COMMUNICATIVE ACTIVITY 4

Have I Got That Right?

Part 1: On your own, fill in the chart below with information about yourself and four of your classmates. See how much you can remember about your classmates.

Name	Favourite Sport	Places Visited	Favourite Food	Hobbies	Present or Future Career
1.					
2.					
3.					
4.					

Part 2: Work as a class. Take turns choosing classmates and asking them questions about the categories in the chart. You think you know the answer, but you want confirmation. Try to vary the verbs and tenses you use.

Mikhail, you're a soccer fan, aren't you?

Dorothy, you love peanut butter, don't you?

Sara, you've decided to become an engineer, haven't you?

BRINGING IT ALL TOGETHER

✳ COMMUNICATIVE ACTIVITY 5

The Life and Work of Franz Mesmer

Look at the picture. What is happening? How much do you know about hypnotism? The person whose ideas paved the way for modern hypnotism was Franz Mesmer. Working with a partner, decide which questions you would like to ask about Mesmer's life and work. Write these questions, then use the Internet to find the answers.
Share your information with your class.

	Question	Answer
1	Where was he born?	Iznang, Germany
2		
3		
4		
5		
6		

Reading

Read the passage and answer the questions that follow.

HYPNOSIS HELPS WOMAN QUIT SMOKING

By Jane Lima, *The Daily Planet*

A 50-year-old woman who has been chain-smoking since the age of 18 has finally been cured of her <u>addiction</u> with the help of <u>hypnosis</u>. Karen Bourne of Thunder Bay, Ontario, took the unusual step of contacting a hypnotist after watching a television program about the uses of hypnosis. I spoke to Karen at her home.

The Planet: Karen, tell me about your history with smoking. When did you start? How many cigarettes a day did you smoke?

Karen: Well, I first tried it when I was 17, and by the time I was 18 I was addicted. Smoking is like that, isn't it? Once you start, it's hard to stop. At my worst point, I was smoking two packs per day.

The Planet: Have you tried to quit before?

Karen: Yes, I have. I've tried cutting down, and I've tried going <u>cold turkey</u>. I've tried gum, patches, and herbal medicines. Nothing worked. My kids used to say, "Mom, do you want to die of a heart attack or lung cancer before you're 50?" No, I didn't. I had to do something.

The Planet: What made you decide to try hypnosis?

Karen: I watched a program on TV about it. I learned all about how it was started in the 1700s by an Austrian doctor called Franz Mesmer. That's where we get the word "<u>mesmerize</u>" from. He believed the universe was filled with an <u>invisible</u> magnetic <u>fluid</u> that connected people to the planets and to each other. Mesmer thought the motion of the planets influenced the fluid, which then influenced people's health.

The Planet: What did he do?

Karen: He believed the magnetic fluid could be transferred between people. He used to put people in a <u>trance</u>, and then sit close to them or touch them for a long time. People claimed they felt better after a treatment.

The Planet: But that's all nonsense, isn't it? We know better today, don't we?

Karen: I'm not sure. Modern science has found no evidence of invisible fluids or channels or energy centres, but there is plenty of evidence that being mesmerized, or hypnotized, is helpful for a lot of conditions. It's especially useful for people who have <u>phobias</u> or addictions.

The Planet: When I think of hypnosis, I usually imagine an entertainer putting a member of the audience into a trance and making her eat an onion, or do something silly. This is quite different, isn't it?

Karen: Yes, it is. This is medical hypnosis. It's more like a science. I was <u>skeptical</u> before I tried it, but I had nothing to lose.

> *The Planet*: Tell me about your treatment. How long did it take you to quit smoking?
> Karen: One session! It was so quick and easy. I haven't had a cigarette in five months now, and I have never felt better—or richer! I'd recommend this to anyone!
> *The Planet*: Thank you for talking to me, Karen, and congratulations!

COMPREHENSION

Write complete sentences to answer the questions below.

1. How long did Karen smoke? How many cigarettes per day did she smoke?

   _____

2. Which methods had Karen already tried to help her quit smoking?

   _____

3. Who warned Karen that she might die of a heart attack or lung cancer?

   _____

4. According to Franz Mesmer, what kind of fluid was the universe filled with?

   _____

5. Has modern science found any evidence that this fluid exists? (Use a short answer.)

   _____

6. If you are afraid of heights or small spaces, could hypnosis help you?

   _____

7. Karen was certain that hypnosis was going to cure her addiction. True or false?

   _____

8. How many sessions with the hypnotist did Karen need?

   _____

Listening

🔊 *Track 10*

WHICH APARTMENT SHOULD WE RENT?

Listen to the audio.

COMPREHENSION

Answer the following questions. Write complete sentences.

1. How many apartments did Angela and Emily see at the complex on Pinehurst Avenue?

    _____

2. Which apartment did they prefer?

    _____

3. What is the view from the ninth floor apartment on Pinehurst Avenue?

    _____

4. What can you see from the apartment on the fifth floor of the Oakville Avenue complex?

    _____

5. Is there indoor parking at the Oakville Avenue complex? (Use a short answer.)

    _____

6. How much extra a month does the indoor parking cost?

    _____

7. How old is the apartment complex on Oakville Avenue?

    _____

8. Has it been well maintained? (Use a short answer.)

    _____

9. Are the utilities included in the rent for the apartment on Oakville Avenue? (Use a short answer.)

    _____

10. Is the cable included in the rent at Oakville Avenue? (Use a short answer.)

    _____

11. Are the women happy to be moving? (Use a short answer.)

    _____

Writing

Listen to the conversation between Emily and Angela again. Now, read the comprehension questions and your answers.

Write a short composition (200 words) about the apartment you would like to live in. You may use the examples from the conversation between Emily and Angela or simply use your imagination.

CHAPTER REVIEW

Summary

Three kinds of questions are addressed in this chapter:

- **Yes / no (interrogative) questions.** These are very simple, and expect the answer "yes" or "no." Short answers (e.g., "Yes, I did.") are used; these are more polite than a simple *yes* or *no*.

- **Negative Questions.** These use negative forms to get confirmation from the listener, often in a situation we are surprised about.

- **Information questions.** These start with the words *who*, *what*, *where*, *when*, *why*, and *how*. Use these when you need specific information.

- **Tag questions.** Use these when you want your listener to confirm something you think is true.

EXERCISE 1

Change each of the following statements into yes / no questions. Remember to add the question mark at the end of the question.

He writes to his mother every week. → Does he write to his mother every week?

1. We will be able to jog in the park later.

   _____

2. I have taught English for six years.

   _____

3. He should arrive on the next train.

   _____

4. The star of the show refused an interview.

    _____

5. The boss wanted to send the information last night.

    _____

EXERCISE 2

Complete the following short answers.

Did Paul go to the mall yesterday? → Yes, he did.

1. Has she seen that movie? No, _____

2. Does the teacher know about the change in schedule? Yes, _____

3. Should we call security? Yes, _____

4. Will the children call their parents? No, _____

5. Are we watching a movie in class today? Yes, _____

EXERCISE 3

Change each of the following statements into a negative question. Remember to contract the verb and add the question mark at the end of the question.

He has written his parents → Hasn't he written his parents?

1. They are talking to the superintendent of the building.

    _____

2. The cable and the hydro are included in the rent.

    _____

3. Hypnotism is a fascinating topic to read about.

    _____

4. Dogs are more interesting than cats.

    _____

5. They will travel to Europe in the spring.

    _____

EXERCISE 4

Change each of the following sentences to an information question. The information you want to ask about is **bolded** and <u>underlined</u>.

I learned <u>**French**</u> in primary school. → What did you learn in primary school?

1. We will see **an eclipse of the moon** tonight.

   _____

2. He took driving lessons **last year**.

   _____

3. You were late for class **because of the accident on the highway**.

   _____

4. He has studied **at the university** for six years.

   _____

5. She met **her husband** while she was travelling.

   _____

EXERCISE 5

Write correct tag questions for each of the following.

She has to resign her job at the college, <u>**doesn't she**</u>?

1. You haven't had your medication yet, _____?

2. He made that suggestion, _____?

3. She is a teacher, _____?

4. People have left for the concert, _____?

5. They couldn't fix my car in time, _____?

Prepositions and Phrasal Verbs

PART 2

7 COMBINING CLAUSES

8 PRESENT PERFECT

9 MODALS

10 TYPES OF QUESTIONS AND SHORT ANSWERS

11 PREPOSITIONS AND PHRASAL VERBS

12 PAST PERFECT AND CONDITIONALS

OVERVIEW

- Prepositions add meaning when we use them with other words. This chapter will examine prepositions of time and space.

- Phrasal verbs are two- or three-word verbs that have a particular meaning when used together. Phrasal verbs consist of a verb and a particle (a preposition or an adverb).

- Some common verbs are *come*, *take*, *put*, *go*, *make*, and *give*. Common particles are *out*, *by*, *up*, *off*, *down*, *over*, and *away*. When we combine these, we get verbs such as *give away*, *make up*, *take off*, *put on*, and *go over*. These verbs have special meanings. It is impossible to know the meaning of these by just looking at the parts.

- For some phrasal verbs, pronouns and other words can come between the parts, but other phrasal verbs must keep all their parts together.

PREPOSITIONS OF TIME

Warm-up

Complete these sentences with *in*, *on*, or *at*.

He is _____ time for his test.

The student is **on** time for his test.

His test starts _____ 9:00.

His birthday is _____ the summer.

He was born _____ July 7, 1996.

Formation

Usually prepositions of time are placed after the verb and before the words they give information about.

Preposition	Use	Example Sentences
in	months, seasons, years, decades, and centuries time of day: in the morning, afternoon, etc.	He was born **in** April. Cherry blossoms come out **in** the spring. Roller skating was popular **in** the seventies. It gets cooler **in** the evening.
at	hours, times of the day, and holidays	The train leaves **at** 8:00 AM. The bats come out **at** night. Are you going away **at** Christmas?
on	days and dates	My driving exam is **on** Wednesday. Canada Day is celebrated **on** July 1.
before / after	indicates time in relation to an event	I'll call you **before** school. He goes to the gym **after** work.
during	used with a period of time (a noun)	**During** his stay, he visited all the tourist sites.
for	used to show how long	He stayed with his family in Halifax **for** two weeks.
until	used to show when an event stops	He stayed **until** the end of his vacation.
by	used with a deadline	His test results should be here **by** tomorrow.
between	used for a time that has a beginning and an end	The parcel will arrive **between** 9:00 AM and 5:00 PM on Wednesday.

EXERCISE 1

Match the first half of each sentence to the second half. Fill in the blanks in the first column with the correct letter from the second column.

1. It rained _____

2. I have an appointment _____

3. Please hand in your assignments _____

4. We travelled by boat _____

5. Leave the lights _____

6. They are getting married _____

a) on till the morning.
b) for seven days and seven nights.
c) in the beautiful month of June.
d) for two weeks, and then we took the train.
e) by early next week, or you will have marks deducted.
f) on April 3 to see the dentist.

EXERCISE 2

Circle the correct prepositions to complete the following sentences.

1. The sun rises (in / on / at) the morning, and the sun sets (in / on / at) the evening.

2. I take the bus every morning (in / on / at) 8:15 AM.

3. They plan to leave (in / on / at) the fifth of this month.

4. The mail always arrives (in / on / at) the afternoon.

5. The neighbour is dropping by (in / on / at) dinnertime.

EXERCISE 3

Fill in the blanks with the correct prepositions. Choose from *at*, *on*, *after*, *for*, *until*, *during*, *by*, or *between*. Use each preposition only once.

1. _____ the famine, many people starved to death.

2. The nurse came to check up on me _____ the doctor left.

3. Many schools celebrate World Teachers' Day _____ October 5 every year.

4. My aunt and uncle came to visit us _____ the end of December.

5. We talked non-stop _____ three hours.

6. They can only stay _____ Sunday night.

7. It is a good idea to have a healthy snack _____ breakfast and lunch.

8. _____ spring the tree will be full of blossoms.

PREPOSITIONS OF PLACE

Warm-up

These two pictures are of a student's dorm room on campus. The picture on the left shows his room before his parents called to say that they were coming to visit. The picture on the right shows his room after he tidied his room for their visit.

Look at the two pictures and talk to your partner about how they are different. Use the example as a guide.

> There was garbage on the floor. After the phone call, there is no garbage on the floor.

Formation

Prepositions can give information about place and indicate exactly where something is located in relation to something else. Prepositions of place are usually placed after the verb.

Preposition	Example Sentences
at	The children are **at** school. She's **at** the mall every Saturday.
in	The sandwiches are **in** the lunch box. The spoons are **in** the drawer.
on /off	The cat is **on** the roof. The cat jumped **off** the roof.
into	The teacher suddenly came **into** the room. Go **into** the house through the back door.

Continued

Preposition	Example Sentences
between	The sugar is **between** the coffee and the tea. She stood **between** her mother and her father.
among	The pear tree is standing alone **among** all the apple trees in the orchard.
in front of / behind	There is a parking space **in front of** the house. The backyard is **behind** the house.
above / below	The sky **above** her was filled with clouds. The ground **below** them was muddy.
over / under	Wear your coat **over** your sweater; you'll be warmer. Wear your sweater **under** your coat; you'll be warmer.
next to / beside	My car is parked **next to** the yellow car. Please come and sit **beside** me.
by / near	Her purse is **by** her chair on the floor. Their dorm is **near** the library.
across from / opposite	They sat **across from** each other at the dinner table. The building **opposite** the bank is now a clothing store.
inside / outside	The cat always stays **inside** the house, and the dog always plays **outside** the house.
through	Drive **through** this tunnel and you'll get to the highway. They passed **through** town on their way to the mountain.

EXERCISE 4

Fill in the blanks with the correct prepositions. Choose from *at, in, on, off, into, between, among, in front of, behind, over, under, next to, by, beside, above, below, across, inside, outside,* or *through.* You can use a preposition more than once.

1. The keys are _____ my pocket.

2. His gold pen is _____ the many expensive pens he has on his desk.

3. Do you see the bike trying to pass _____ the car and the van?

4. Come and sit right _____ me; I'll be able to hear you better.

5. Come and sit _____ from me; I'll be able to see you better.

6. Something smells good. I wonder what's cooking _____ the pot; I want to look _____ the lid.

7. _____ the tour bus, it was 40 degrees and raining hard.

8. We have to go outside; we can't stay _____ this crowded house all day.

❖ COMMUNICATIVE ACTIVITY 1

Missing Pen

Your teacher has hidden a pen somewhere inside the classroom. One by one, take turns trying to guess the location of the pen. Use prepositions in your questions.

I think the pen is under the desk.

I think the pen is inside the pencil case.

❖ COMMUNICATIVE ACTIVITY 2

Hiding Place

Work in pairs. Discuss this problem with your partner: You have a housemate who always eats your cookies. Where in the kitchen can you hide your cookies?

Use the words in the list with prepositions to describe good places to hide cookies.

oven	cabinet	plate	toaster	dish rack
refrigerator	box	cup	chair	garbage can
cupboard	jar	drawer	table	detergent
pantry	microwave	counter	plant	

Now continue the same activity. This time, your housemate always borrows your jeans without asking. Where in the house can you hide your jeans from him or her?

PHRASAL VERBS PART 1

Warm-up

Discuss the following questions in pairs.

- What time do you usually get up in the morning?
- How late do you stay up in the evenings?
- Have you taken up any new hobbies lately?
- What is the best way to make up with someone after an argument?

Formation

Phrasal verbs contain a verb and a preposition, or a verb and an adverb. Each combination creates a unique meaning. When the preposition or adverb changes, so does the meaning.

Below are some common phrasal verbs that use the verbs *get*, *put*, *look*, and *take*.

Get		Put	
Phrasal Verb	**Example Sentence**	**Phrasal Verb**	**Example Sentence**
get up	I **get up** at 6:00 every morning.	put on (1)	Why don't you **put on** your glasses?
get in	I want to **get in**; could you open the door please?	put on (2)	She isn't really crying. She's just **putting** it **on** to get your sympathy.
get on / get off	They **get on** (**off**) the bus at 7:00 A.M.	put off (1)	We've postponed the wedding twice already; we can't **put** it **off** any longer.
get over	Her boyfriend left her, and she didn't **get over** him for a whole year.	put off (2)	Don't be **put off** by this month's sales; this is just a minor setback.
get out of	I want to **get out of** this business; it isn't making any money.	put out	The firefighters **put out** the fire very quickly.
get down	The children like to climb the trees but have difficulty when they have to **get down** again.	put away	Can you **put** the groceries **away** in the cupboard?
get behind in	Don't **get behind in** your reading, or you'll be confused in class.	put up with	She treats him horribly; I don't know why he **puts up with** her.

Look		Take	
Phrasal Verb	**Example Sentence**	**Phrasal Verb**	**Example Sentence**
look up	I need to **look up** this word in the dictionary to see what it means.	take up (1)	I want to **take up** the piano; may I have lessons?
look after	Can you **look after** my cat while I'm on vacation?	take up (2)	The teacher said he would **take up** the homework, so we can understand it better.
look for	Are you **looking for** your phone? Here it is.	take off (1)	The plane **takes off** at 4:00 PM.

Continued

Look		Take	
Phrasal Verb	**Example Sentence**	**Phrasal Verb**	**Example Sentence**
look out	**Look out!** There's a car coming!	take off (2)	Please **take off** your shoes before you come in.
look in on	I've left my kids alone in the house. Can you **look in on** them at dinner time?	take in (1)	Those pants are too big for you; you should **take in** 10 cm at the waist so they fit better.
look down on	Don't **look down on** him just because he isn't as rich as you are!	take in (2)	She **took in** the stray cat and adopted it as her pet.
look away	The result of the game is on the TV screen. If you don't want to see it, **look away** now.	take after	She **takes after** her mother; they are both very artistic.
look forward to	Are you **looking forward to** your summer vacation?	take down	The landlord asked the tenant to **take down** all the posters from the wall.
look up to	The boy **looks up to** his father and wants to be like him.	take on	The clerk **took on** extra work as his new project.

EXERCISE 5

Fill in the blanks with the correct phrasal verbs to complete the sentences. Use the items from the list below. There are more choices than questions.

take in	put off	get up	get down	take up
look in on	put up with	take down	get on	looking forward to

1. _____ from that ladder! It isn't safe!

2. We've _____ the party for three weeks. Let's have it on Saturday.

3. Can you _____ my dog while I'm at work?

4. What time do you _____ the bus every evening?

5. The tree is too tall and dangerous. We need to _____ it _____ before it falls.

6. Are you _____ your graduation?

EXERCISE 6

Replace the **bolded**, <u>underlined</u> part of the following sentences with a phrasal verb from the chart on pages 215 and 216. You may need to change some of the verb forms.

1. I **<u>get out of bed</u>** every morning at 6:30 AM.

   _____

2. He **<u>is very similar to</u>** his father.

   _____

3. If you're hot, why don't you **<u>remove</u>** your coat?

   _____

4. I'll call you right before the plane **<u>departs</u>**.

   _____

5. When you've finished using the hammer, can you please **<u>put it in its correct place</u>**?

   _____

6. If you can't **<u>extinguish</u>** the bonfire yourself, you'll need to call the fire department.

   _____

7. I am always stressed. I think I should **<u>start doing</u>** yoga.

   _____

8. I'm **<u>trying to find</u>** my car keys. Have you seen them?

   _____

COMMUNICATIVE ACTIVITY 3

Who Might Say It?

A. Work with a partner. Match each of the following statements with the person who might make that statement. Fill in the blanks in the first column with the correct letter from the second column.

1. I'm really looking forward to sitting on the beach for two weeks. I'm exhausted. _____

2. You can't get behind in your studies this term. You already have several low grades on your record. _____

3. I don't know why you put up with him. He treats you like garbage! You don't need him! _____

a) someone who has a job and a family, and who volunteers with three different charities

b) someone who has been working very hard and who badly needs a break

c) a young man who thinks his girlfriend's parents don't like him because he isn't well educated

d) a school counsellor talking to a student who has some problems with time management

4. I'm sorry. I can't take on anything else. I have too many commitments already. _____

5. Your younger brother and sister really look up to you. You need to set a good example. _____

6. I always feel that your family looks down on me. It isn't my fault that I don't make a lot of money. _____

e) a young woman trying to persuade her best friend to leave her boyfriend

f) a parent speaking to the oldest child, who has been getting into trouble a lot recently

B. With the same partner, prepare a dialogue using one of the six sentences. Make sure the sentence appears somewhere in your conversation. Share your dialogue with the class.

PHRASAL VERBS PART 2 (SEPARABLE AND NON-SEPARABLE VERBS)

Warm-up

Work in pairs, and read the sentences below. Imagine the situation. What might the person say next? Choose an appropriate verb and preposition from the following list. Create the next sentence, using the pronoun *it*.

Verbs: pick   turn   put

Prepositions: on   up   down   off

I love that song! **Turn it up!**

1. The light is hurting my eyes.

_____

2. Your dirty shirt is on the floor again.

_____

3. Be careful! That knife is dangerous.

_____

4. I can't hear you with that loud music playing.

_____

5. It's too dark in here. Why is that lamp off?

_____

Formation

SEPARABLE PHRASAL VERBS

The parts of some phrasal verbs can sometimes be separated by a noun or pronoun when used in a sentence. The following chart lists some separable phrasal verbs.

Phrasal Verb		Example Sentences
Verb + Preposition (+ object)	Verb + Pronoun + Preposition	
point out (someone)	point her / him / them out	The girl **pointed out** the clowns. The girl **pointed** them **out**.
check out (something)	check it out	Let's **check out** the new store. Let's **check** it **out**.
turn on / up / down / off (something)	turn it on; turn it up; turn it down; turn it off	**Turn up** the radio. **Turn** it **up**. **Turn on** your laptop. **Turn** it **on**.
bring up (something)	bring it up	**Bring up** your concern at the meeting, and we can talk about it. **Bring** it **up** at the meeting.
throw out (something)	throw it out	Don't **throw out** your old clothes. Don't **throw** them **out**.

NON-SEPARABLE PHRASAL VERBS

Other phrasal verbs must not be separated by their pronoun. The preposition must always follow the verb. The following chart shows a list of common phrasal verbs that never split.

Phrasal Verb		Example Sentences
Verb + Preposition	Verb + Preposition + Object	
catch up on	catch up on something	I have to **catch up on** my homework. I have to **catch up on** it.
catch up with	catch up with someone	I have to **catch up with** my friends. I have to **catch up with** them.
go over	go over something	We need to **go over** last month's bills. We need to **go over** them.

Continued

Phrasal Verb		Example Sentences
Verb + Preposition	**Verb + Preposition + Object**	
run out of	run out of something	We've **run out of** milk. We've **run out of** it.
take after	take after someone	He **takes after** his dad. He **takes after** him.
look after	look after something or someone	The children are **looking after** their grandfather. They are **looking after** him.

See Appendix D for a longer list of separable and non-separable phrasal verbs.

EXERCISE 7

Fill in the blanks with an appropriate preposition to complete the phrasal verb. Use the words from the list.

over	out	after	out	up	off

1. Please look _____ my pets while I'm away.

2. The tax auditor was going _____ the shopkeeper's income.

3. Don't throw them _____. We can recycle them.

4. We should turn _____ all the lights before we sleep.

5. The secretary put it on the agenda and brought it _____ at the meeting.

6. Can you point _____ the new IT manager if you see her?

BRINGING IT ALL TOGETHER

COMMUNICATIVE ACTIVITY 4

Role Play

Work in pairs. Your teacher will give each group a card. Look at the situation on the card, and create a two-minute role play. Somewhere in the role play, you must use the phrasal verb on the card.

Share your role play with the class. Your classmates must guess what your phrasal verb is, so don't make it too easy!

Tell Us About . . .

Work in groups of four. Your teacher will give you two dice. Take turns throwing the dice. For each number you throw, tell your group about that topic.

1	2	3	4	5	6
	something you got behind in	someone you look up to	something you threw out, and you wish you still had	someone you don't really like, but that you put up with	someone you take after

7	8	9	10	11	12
something you never remember and always have to look up	something you always run out of	someone who looked after you as a child	something you want your teacher to go over again	something you are looking forward to	something you lost, looked for, and never found

Reading

Read the passage and answer the questions that follow.

THE LOST PHONE

Mei has always been a bit <u>messy</u> and <u>absent-minded</u>. On her sixteenth birthday, Mei got the smartphone that she had always wanted. Her mother was a bit concerned because Mei had lost her two previous phones. "You need to look after your things," she told Mei. "You take after your father; he is always losing things, too. You need to put things away properly."

Mei looked up to her mother, and she knew her mother was right. She promised to make sure she wouldn't lose her new <u>cherished</u> treasure. Only a week after receiving her gift, however, she misplaced it! Mei was devastated and looked for it everywhere. She had an <u>inkling</u> that it was in the house somewhere. She called her sister Lian and her brother Jun to help her look all over the house. They spent most of Saturday morning looking everywhere. Jun looked under the beds, inside the closets, inside the pockets of jackets, and underneath and behind all the furniture.

Lian looked in front of and around the side tables, armchairs, and sofa in the living room. Then she went to the kitchen and not only looked inside all the cabinets but even looked inside the refrigerator. She went through the <u>pile</u> of magazines on a chair, just in case the phone was between the papers. There was no phone anywhere.

Continued

Mei would have called her own phone to hear the ring tone and locate it, but she knew that her phone battery was dead and the phone would not ring. She <u>paced</u> back and forth in the basement nervously wondering what she could have done with her phone. Where could she have left it? Had she put it down somewhere and forgotten it? She kept walking in circles and biting her nails as she became more and more nervous. Finally she called her <u>siblings</u> and they sat down in the dining room to talk about the lost phone.

"Mei, I'm really tired of you losing your things. We have spent our whole morning looking and looking for it. Can't you remember where you used the phone last?" Lian asked as they sat disappointed around the table.

Jun said, "Let's go over the last few hours. Who was your last call from?"

"It was from Mom. She called me to remind me of my piano lesson today. Oh my! I forgot to practise the piano! I'm going to get behind with my lessons!"

"Let's focus here." Jun told Mei. "That's your problem, Mei: you're not focused. Now, where were you when Mom called you to remind you of your piano lesson?"

"I was in the laundry room about to wash my soccer uniform, and . . . Oh no! I think the phone is in the laundry room, in the basement!" Mei exclaimed and ran down the stairs in a <u>panic</u>. She went straight to the laundry room and opened the dryer and pulled out all her clothes and in the middle of the clothes was indeed her phone!

"How on earth could you put your phone in the dryer?" Lian asked, puzzled.

"Well . . . I was talking to Mom at the same time that I was putting my clothes in the dryer and I guess I must have thrown the phone in with the clothes when I was done talking."

Lian and Jun breathed deeply and shook their heads in amazement.

Mei breathed a <u>sigh of relief</u> when she turned on her phone and found that it was still working. Jun and Lian were looking at her with discontent. Finally Lian said, "Oh Mei, Mei, when are you ever going to stop doing such <u>goofy</u> things?"

COMPREHENSION

Answer the following questions. Use complete sentences.

1. Who does Mei take after? Why?

   _____

2. When did Mei lose her phone?

   _____

3. Who helped her to look for it?

   _____

4. Name some of the places they looked for the phone.

   _____

5. When they sat down to talk, how did Jun feel? How did Lian feel?

   _____

6. Why did Mei run down the stairs?

   _____

7. What happened when Mei turned on her phone?

   _____

DISCUSSION

Discuss the following questions in pairs.

1. Have you ever lost something precious? How did you feel?

2. Where are some obvious places to look if you lose the following?

   - keys
   - coffee cup
   - USB key for your computer
   - pen
   - wallet

Listening

◀)) *Track 11*

EAT HEALTHY, LIVE WELL

Listen to the audio of a radio program.

COMPREHENSION

Answer the following questions. Write complete sentences.

1. Where is Dr. Nilsson from?

   _____

2. What are the two sections of his book about?

   _____

3. What is the problem the first caller is having?

   _____

4. What advice does Dr. Nilsson give to the second caller?

   _____

5. When does the book come out?

   _____

Listen to the audio a second time. Which of the following sentences or phrases did you hear?

1. a) . . . talking about his new book, *Eat Healthy, Live Well.*
    b) . . . talking on his new book, *Eat Healthy, Live Well.*

2. a) Well, we're very excited to have you over our show this morning.
    b) Well, we're very excited to have you on our show this morning

3. a) Let's start off with the first part of the book then.
    b) Let's start with the first part of the book then.

4. a) If you could sum up . . .
    b) If you could sum off . . .

5. a) In my research I came across Canada's Food Guide.
    b) In my research I came beside Canada's Food Guide.

6. a) I have made up charts that give suggested diets for different body types and lifestyles.
    b) I have made out charts that give suggested diets for different body types and lifestyles.

7. a) I keep going off diets and nothing works.
    b) I keep going on diets and nothing works.

8. a) Try taking out a team sport instead of just heading over to the gym.
    b) Try taking up a team sport instead of just heading out to the gym.

In the following chart, list the phrasal verbs you heard that are new, and guess their meaning.

Phrasal Verb	Meaning

Writing

Write a short composition (75 words) in response to ONE of the following questions. Note that each question uses phrasal verbs. Use phrasal verbs in your responses.

1. Do you get along with your siblings and your friends?

2. Who in your family do you take after, and in what ways?

3. Have you ever taken up and then given up an activity?

Summary

- Prepositions often give information about time and space. Prepositions of time tell us when something happens or happened. Prepositions of place tell us the location or position of a person or object.

- Phrasal verbs consist of a verb + preposition or verb + adverb. When put together, these words have a particular meaning.

- If the parts of a phrasal verb can have a word come between them, the verb is called "separable." When the parts of a phrasal verb must stay together in the sentence, then the verb is called "non-separable."

EXERCISE 1

Fill in the blanks with the correct preposition of time or space.

1. The train is late again! It is never _____ time lately.

2. The man standing _____ the door is the bouncer.

3. Her birthday is _____ October.

4. Please place the flowers _____ the table.

5. The mother hid the candies _____ top of the refrigerator.

EXERCISE 2

Look at the pictures and suggest advice. Use the words from the list.

| get up slowly | get over | go over | get off carefully |

1. _____

2. _____

3. _____

4. _____

EXERCISE 3

Decide which of the following sentences have **separable** phrasal verbs and which have **non-separable** ones. Write **S** for separable and **NS** for non-separable in the blank after each sentence.

1. I don't like to take up dangerous sports. _____

2. If you give up on your dreams, then you're a quitter. _____

3. We have gone over this problem before. _____

4. Always look up information about any company you want to purchase from. _____

EXERCISE 4

Circle the correct preposition to complete the phrasal verb in each of the following sentences.

1. Johnny asked (**up / for / over**) a new computer for his birthday.

2. Sarah missed school this week. She has to catch (**up / for / through / in**) on her school work.

3. My flight to England takes (**away / off / up**) at 8:35 PM and lands at 7:15 the next morning.

4. The baseball player made (**over / up / from / away**) some excuse for missing practice.

5. It is good to get (**up / from / over**) failures and learn from our mistakes.

PART 2

7 COMBINING CLAUSES

8 PRESENT PERFECT

9 MODALS

10 TYPES OF QUESTIONS AND SHORT ANSWERS

11 PREPOSITIONS AND PHRASAL VERBS

12 PAST PERFECT AND CONDITIONALS

12 Past Perfect and Conditionals

OVERVIEW

Past Perfect

- We use the past perfect verb tense to refer to events that started and finished in the past. It includes two words: *had* + a past participle.

- The past perfect and the simple past are often used together, in the same sentence, to describe past actions. The past perfect describes the past action that occurred first in the past, and the simple past refers to the past action that occurred afterwards:

  When I arrived at the theatre, the movie had already started.

  Sue didn't want to see the movie; she had already seen it.

Conditionals

- A conditional sentence shows a relationship between two actions. It is a two-part sentence: the *if* clause (the condition) and the main clause (the result). The speaker is saying that if action or situation A occurs, then action or situation B is the result.

- In English, there are three types of conditional sentences. Conditional 1 and Conditional 2 refer to events in the present or the near future.

  - Conditional 1: If I have money, I will buy a lottery ticket.

    This refers to an event that is likely to occur in the present or the near future.

- Conditional 2: If I had money, I would buy a lottery ticket.

    This refers to an event that is not likely to occur in the present or the near future.

- Conditional 3 refers to events that could have occurred in the past, but did not.

    If I had had money, I would have bought a lottery ticket.

    The speaker wants to express a different outcome that could have happened. Here, the speaker did not have money so was unable to buy a lottery ticket. It is now too late.

PAST PERFECT

Warm-up

Complete the following sentences:

Before I { started studying here, came to Canada, was 18, left school, } I had never { seen tried eaten played } _____.

Then I { saw it, tried it, ate it, played it, } and it was _____.

Before I came to Canada, I had never seen snow. Then I saw it, and it was horrible!

Work in groups of three. Share your sentences.

Formation

The simple past tense is used to describe an event that occurred in the more recent past. You use the past perfect to talk about an action that occurred *before* this past action. This establishes a timeline to understand in what order actions in the past happened.

The past perfect tense is a two-word verb: the past of the auxiliary verb *have* (*had*) + the past participle of the main/action verb.

I turned on the television at 2:00 PM, but the soccer match **had started** at 1:00.

First, the soccer match started.
Then, I turned on the television.

My roommate **had promised** me she would tidy the apartment, but when I came home it was still untidy.

First, she promised me that she would tidy the apartment.
Then, I came home.

I **had planned** to major in Economics, but when I took a Business course, I changed my mind.

First, I planned to major in Economics.
Then, I took a Business course.

Note that the adverbs *already* and *just* are commonly used with the past perfect. When you use *already* and *just*, put them between the auxiliary verb *had* and the main verb.

Paul jumped. Something **had just moved** in the bushes beside him.

We **had already left** for class when he arrived.

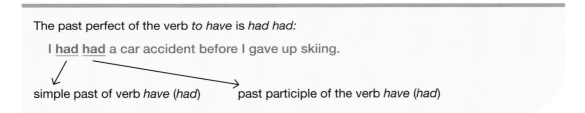

The past perfect of the verb *to have* is *had had:*

I **had had** a car accident before I gave up skiing.

simple past of verb *have* (*had*)   past participle of the verb *have* (*had*)

EXERCISE 1

Work with a partner. Complete the following chart with the correct forms of each verb.

Base Form	Simple Past	Past Perfect
talk	talked	had talked
	flew	
		had written
	called	
sing		
think		
		had cried
teach		

Continued

Base Form	Simple Past	Past Perfect
	walked	
buy		
		had brought
	saw	
pay		
	knew	

EXERCISE 2

Your choice of verb tenses in a sentence often changes the meaning of the sentence. With a partner, compare the following pairs of sentences. Do (a) and (b) have the same meaning, or is the meaning different? Discuss any differences you find.

1. a) When they heard the news, they left the restaurant.
    b) When they heard the news, they had left the restaurant.

    Comments: _____

2. a) When he was 10, he had already published three short novels.
    b) When he was 10, he published three short novels.

    Comments: _____

3. a) The students completed the assignment at the end of class.
    b) The students had completed the assignment before the end of class.

    Comments: _____

4. a) When Cheryl came home from work, Chris made dinner.
    b) When Cheryl came home from work, Chris had made dinner.

    Comments: _____

5. a) When the ambulance arrived at the hospital, the patient had recovered.
    b) When the ambulance arrived at the hospital, the patient recovered.

    Comments: _____

EXERCISE 3

Fill in the blanks using the past perfect of the verbs in parentheses.

He slammed on the brakes. The child **had already run** into the street.

1. I wanted to buy my daughter the shoes but she _____ just

    _____ (pay) for them.

2. The news surprised her. She _____ (think) the store was open.

3. When the bell rang, the students _____ already _____ (leave) the schoolyard.

4. Anna screamed. The noise _____ (frighten) her.

5. After the vandals _____ (run away), the police arrived.

EXERCISE 4

After living abroad for many years, Marina returned to the town where she had grown up. Many things had changed. Fill in the blanks in the following sentences describing the changes. Use the past perfect of the verbs in parentheses.

1. Thanks to a large new housing development, the population _____ (grow) to 30,000.

2. There was a big new shopping mall. It _____ (open) in 2010.

3. Marina's old neighbours _____ (sell) their house. They _____ (move) to the coast.

4. The nicest hotel in town _____ (become) a home for senior citizens.

5. Marina went to visit her favourite teacher, but sadly, she _____ (die).

6. Even her old high school wasn't there. It _____ (burn down) two years earlier.

✥ COMMUNICATIVE ACTIVITY 1

Two Sides to Every Story

Reiko, Finn, and Jody have each requested meetings with the heads of their college departments to complain about a professor. Work in groups of three. Read their situations, and choose one. Role-play the conversation that takes place with the student, the professor, and the department head. What solution do you think the department head would reach in each case?

Situation 1.

Reiko: My professor had promised me I could have an extension until Monday, but when I went to his office to hand in my paper, he refused to accept it!

Professor: I had promised Reiko an extension until Monday morning. She showed up in my office at 4:30 in the afternoon.

Situation 2.

Finn: I got a mark of zero for missing a test, but I had already emailed my professor to say I was sick!

Professor: Finn had already missed three tests because of "illness." I decided to ignore his latest email.

Situation 3.

Jody: I got an F grade on my transcript for Math 101. I had dropped the course two months earlier.

Professor: Jody had not officially withdrawn from the course; she had simply stopped coming. That doesn't count as a withdrawal.

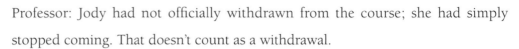

CONDITIONALS

Warm-up

Work with a partner. Partner A poses general questions with *if* and Partner B answers. Then switch roles. Structure the general questions along these lines:

> If you **forget to water your plants**, what will happen?
>
> If people **don't look both ways before they cross a street**, what will happen?
>
> If we **don't hand in our assignments on time**, what will happen?

Formation

Conditional sentences have two parts, an *if* clause (an incomplete thought) and a main clause (a complete thought).

The *if* clause may come either at the beginning of the sentence (with a comma [,] between the *if* clause and the main clause) or at the end of the sentence (with no comma needed). The meaning is the same.

There are three types of conditionals.

Condition Type	If Clause	Key Word(s)	Main Clause	Structure
1. Conditions that describe probable / possible situations in the present or near future	*If* + simple present tense	*will*	simple future tense	*If* + simple present + comma + simple future
	If he **calls** me, If she **has** the time,		I **will talk** to him. she **will watch** the hockey game.	

Continued

Condition Type	*If* Clause	Key Word(s)	Main Clause	Structure
2. Conditions that describe unlikely situations in the near future	*If* + simple past tense	*would*	*would* + base form of verb	*If* + simple past + comma + *would* + comma + base form of verb
	If he **called** me, If I **found** a wallet on the street, If I **won** the lottery,		I **would talk** to him. I **would return** it. I **would buy** a house.	
3. Conditions that refer to an event in past time that did not happen; the speaker gives a likely result if it had actually happened	*If* + past perfect tense	*would have*	*would have* + past participle	*If* + past perfect + comma + *would* + *have* + past participle
	If he **had called** me, If he **had known** about the party,		I **would have talked** to him. he **would have gone.**	

EXERCISE 5

With a partner, look at the clauses in each column of the following chart and match the *if* clause with the appropriate main clause. Write the complete sentences below the chart.

1. If we are invited to the ceremony,	she will be healthier.
2. If Tom has enough money,	she will not call you.
3. If Alice knows you are not home,	I will not take a taxi.
4. If Sam becomes an architect,	he will buy dinner for all of us.
5. If Sara stops smoking,	I will not drive my children to school.
6. If I am not late,	he will make a lot of money.
7. If it does not rain,	we will go.

_____

_____

_____

_____

_____

_____

EXERCISE 6

Use the rules for probable or possible situations (Conditional 1) to complete the sentences.

If she _____ (have) time, she _____ (watch) the hockey game.

If she **has** time, she **will** watch the hockey game.

simple present   simple future

1. If my friend _____ (**wait**) for me after class, I _____ (**give**) her a ride home.

2. If my children _____ (**eat**) their vegetables, I _____ (**let**) them eat ice cream for dessert.

3. I _____ (**pay**) my bills at the bank if I _____ (**have**) time after work.

4. The bank _____ (**lend**) him money to buy a car if he _____ (**get**) a job.

5. If I _____ (**find**) the missing file, my boss _____ (**be**) happy.

EXERCISE 7

Change each of the following statements into a question.

Statement: If she has the time, she will watch the hockey game.

Question: If she has the time, will she watch the hockey game?

1. If it's warm on Saturday, we'll plant some flowers.

   _____

2. If we hurry, we'll make the seven o'clock show.

   _____

3. If you walk along Maple Street, you'll find a taxi.

   _____

4. You'll be angry if I borrow your leather jacket without asking you.

   _____

5. I'll call the police if they don't turn down their music.

   _____

⁘ COMMUNICATIVE ACTIVITY 2

One Hundred Years From Now . . .

Work with a partner. Think about what life will be like in the future. Complete the following sentences using Conditional 1.

1. If the population of the Earth reaches 10 billion, ⸺⸺⸺⸺⸺⸺.

2. If there is no more oil or gas, ⸺⸺⸺⸺⸺⸺.

3. If scientists find ways to increase the average lifespan, ⸺⸺⸺⸺⸺.

4. If the polar ice caps melt, ⸺⸺⸺⸺⸺⸺.

5. If Canada becomes part of the United States, ⸺⸺⸺⸺⸺.

Share your ideas with your class.

EXERCISE 8

Refer to the chart on page 233 for Conditional 2 (unlikely situations in the near future). Fill in the blanks using the correct form of the verb in parentheses.

If I ⸺⸺⸺ (have) my camera, I ⸺⸺⸺ (take) pictures of the street dancers.

If I **had** my camera, I **would take** pictures of the street dancers.

1. If she ⸺⸺⸺ (sell) her camera on eBay, she ⸺⸺⸺ (get) only $50.00 for it.

2. ⸺⸺⸺ you ⸺⸺⸺ (call) Samantha if I ⸺⸺⸺ (give) you her number?

3. If she ⸺⸺⸺ (quit) smoking, she ⸺⸺⸺ (feel) healthier.

4. I ⸺⸺⸺ (not, run) a marathon if I ⸺⸺⸺ (not, train) first.

5. ⸺⸺⸺ you ⸺⸺⸺ (travel) if you ⸺⸺⸺ (win) the lottery?

6. If Anna ⸺⸺⸺ (go) to bed earlier, she ⸺⸺⸺ (not, be) late for work so often.

EXERCISE 9

Unscramble each group of words on the next page to make sentences. Do not add or change any words, but pay attention to punctuation.

my job / would exercise / quit / If / every day / I

If I quit my job, I would exercise every day.

1. If / to bed earlier / Sophie / went / she / all the time / so tired / would not be

   _____

2. his exam / If / would pass / harder / Paul / studied / he

   _____

3. would not miss / we / If / his call / went / we / home

   _____

4. sick / Samsa / ate / would feel / too much chocolate / she / if

   _____

5. she / it / If / a job / Juliette / offered / the company / would take

   _____

6. Manuel / If / enough money / he / had / a Mexican restaurant / would open

   _____

EXERCISE 10

Imagine these things were true. What would you do? Complete the following sentences.

1. If today were a snow day and all classes were cancelled, I _____

2. If I were a famous sports star, I _____

3. If I lived in Antarctica, I _____

4. If I were 2 m tall, I _____

5. If this were Chinese class instead of English class, we _____

COMMUNICATIVE ACTIVITY 3

What If . . .?

First, use your own ideas to complete the following questions for unlikely situations in the present or the near future.

If you won a free trip, where _____?

If you won a free trip, where would you go?

1. If you did not go to school, how _____

2. If you won money, what _____

3. If you failed your English course, who _____

4. If you witnessed an accident, when _____

5. If you found a wallet in the classroom, where _____

Now, work with a partner. Read each question aloud and write your partner's answer below.

If you won a free trip, where would you go?

If I won a free trip, I would fly to Tuscany and I would rent a villa.

_____

_____

_____

_____

_____

_____

_____

EXERCISE 11

The following sentences refer to past events that did not actually happen. Fill in the blanks with the correct tense of the verbs in parentheses. You will use Conditional 3.

If he _____ (go) to university, he _____ (study) English.

If he **had gone** to university, he **would have studied** English.

1. If they _____ (arrive) earlier, they _____ (see) their friends.

2. If we _____ (not, be) late, we _____ (not, miss) the flight.

3. I _____ (pass) the exam if I _____ (study) harder.

4. If she _____ (not, take) the job, she _____ (go) to Australia.

5. You _____ (be) late if you _____ (not, take) a taxi.

COMMUNICATIVE ACTIVITY 4

If That Had Happened to Me . . .

The following people have all been in embarrassing situations with gifts they have given or received. If you had been in these situations, what would you have done?

Natasha: "I knit a lovely sweater for my cousin. I don't see her very often, and when I gave her the present, I noticed that she had gained about 50 kilos. The sweater was far too small. It was awkward for both of us."

Leo: "Last year, at my birthday party, I started telling my friends how much I hated the local hockey team. Then, I found out that my friends had chipped in to buy me season's tickets to their games! I was so embarrassed!"

Ingrid: "I received a present from my grandmother: a vase shaped like a panda. I don't buy flowers, and I don't like pandas, so I gave it away. When my grandmother visited, she asked where it was. I felt awful."

Khaled: "I helped a classmate move to a new apartment, and as a thank-you gift, my classmate gave me a case of beer. As someone who follows Islam, I don't drink alcohol. I didn't know what to do."

Esra: "My mother told me not to buy her a birthday present because I am a student. I believed her. However, when her birthday came, my brother and sister had presents for her, and I had nothing. I felt terrible. What should I have done?"

BRINGING IT ALL TOGETHER

COMMUNICATIVE ACTIVITY 5

New Year's Resolutions

Do you know what a New Year's resolution is? Do you make New Year's resolutions?

Last year, Roseli had a New Year's resolution to lose weight.

On January 1, she felt optimistic. She said, "If I eat fruit and vegetables, I will lose weight."

On June 30, she had not lost any weight. She felt frustrated. She said, "If I had a buddy, we would support each other."

On December 31, she still had not lost weight. She felt angry and disappointed in herself. She said, "If I had set a specific weight-loss goal, I would have found it easier."

Now write similar sentences for each of the following people:

Simon had a New Year's resolution to launch a dot-com company.

Marjorie had a New Year's resolution to stop buying shoes.

Richard had a New Year's resolution to volunteer at the animal shelter.

YOU had a New Year's resolution to _____.

Reading

Read the following article and answer the questions that follow.

WHY NEW YEAR'S RESOLUTIONS FAIL

Ancient Babylonians promised their gods that they would pay debts and return borrowed items. Romans promised their god Janus, for whom January is named, much the same thing. Many Christians who attend New Year's church services prepare for the New Year with prayers and resolutions. At Jewish New Year, Jews remember past transgressions and sins and then ask for, or grant, forgiveness.

The concept of reflection on past deeds, forgiveness or self-improvement has been present in all religions throughout time.

So the start of the New Year is often the perfect time to turn a new page. If so many people, approximately 50 percent of the population, make New Year's resolutions, why will the majority of them fail? The first few weeks usually go along well, but by February, people are backsliding.

Timothy Pychyl, a professor of psychology at Carleton University in Ottawa, Ontario, says that resolutions are an effort to reinvent oneself. People make resolutions as a way of motivating themselves, says Professor Pychyl. He argues that if people aren't ready to change their habits, particularly their bad habits, this would account for a high failure rate. If people set unrealistic goals and expectations as resolutions, they will not succeed. The other aspect of failed resolutions lies in the cause and effect relationship. You may think if you lose weight, reduce your debts, or exercise more, your entire life will change. If it doesn't, you will get discouraged and then you will revert back to old behaviours.

Making resolutions work is essentially changing behaviour. In order to do that, you have to change your thinking and "rewire" your brain. Habits are created by thinking patterns that create memories. These memories influence your actions when you are faced with a choice or decision. If you try to change this memory by trying to not do it, it will just strengthen it. Change requires creating new memories from new thinking.

So if you make New Year's resolutions, these tips will help you succeed:

1. Focus on one resolution, rather than several.
2. Set realistic specific goals. Losing weight is not a specific goal. Losing 5 kilos in 90 days is a specific goal.
3. Set smaller goals. Take small steps. If the goal is too great, it will require too much of an effort to reach.
4. Have an accountability buddy. If you have a friend to share the goals with, it will be easier to attain the goals by sharing struggles and successes.
5. Celebrate your success when you reach each milestone or goal. If you celebrate each milestone, the final goal will remain possible.
6. Focus your thinking on new behaviours and thought patterns. If you create new memories in your brain, you will successfully change habits.

Continued

7. Focus on the present. What is the one thing you can do today, right now, to reach your goal?
8. If you don't take yourself too seriously, you will have fun and laugh at yourself when you slip. Do not let this slip hold you back from achieving your goal.

Adapted from "Why New Year's Resolutions Fail," by Ray Williams.

COMPREHENSION

Answer the following questions.

1. In what way are modern Christian and Jewish approaches to New Year similar to those of ancient cultures?

   _____

2. What two main questions does this reading answer? (Choose two.)

   a) Why do so many people want to lose weight?
   b) Why do many people fail to keep New Year's resolutions?
   c) If you want your resolutions to succeed, what should you do?
   d) How will your life change if you lose weight, exercise, or get out of debt?

3. Which of the following sentences is NOT true? (Choose one.)

   a) If you are not ready to make a change, you will not succeed.
   b) If your goals are not realistic, you will not succeed.
   c) If you lose weight, your entire life will change.

4. What happens if your weight loss or debt reduction does *not* change your life?

5. Your chances of success are higher if you _____. (Choose **T** for true or **F** for false.)

   a) have many resolutions at the same time **T / F**
   b) set small goals **T / F**
   c) work with a friend **T / F**
   d) focus on the future **T / F**
   e) take yourself seriously **T / F**

Listening

◀)) *Track 12*

RESOLUTIONS!

Listen to the audio of a conversation between two friends in the cafeteria.

COMPREHENSION

Answer the following questions. Write complete sentences.

1. What would Kate have done if she had kept last year's resolutions?

   _____

2. What are Kevin's resolutions this year?

   _____

3. What does Kevin think about his chances of winning the lottery?

   _____

4. What does Kevin think will happen if he and Kate work together on their resolutions?

   _____

5. How has moving into an apartment affected Kate's daily life?

   _____

6. What will help Kevin and Kate to see their progress on a daily basis?

   _____

7. What will they do if they succeed in their goals?

   _____

Writing

Working with a partner, choose one of the following two tasks.

1. Each of you writes down eight things you want to do after you have graduated, reflecting upon what has to happen in each case to make it a reality. Take these ideas and write them as conditional sentences using Conditionals 1 and 2. When you have finished, read aloud to each other and help each other with verb tenses if necessary.

2. Each of you writes down eight things you could have done differently in the past, reflecting upon what could have happened in each case if something had been different. Take your ideas and write them as conditional sentences using Conditional 3. When you have finished, read aloud to each other and help each other with verb tenses if necessary.

Summary

- We use the past perfect to talk about things that happened before another action or event in the past tense. For example, look at the difference between these two sentences:

    When I got home, it started to snow.

    First, I got home; then, it *started* to snow.

    When I got home, it had (already) *started* to snow.

    First, it started to snow; then, I got home. In other words, it started to snow *before* I got home.

- In English, there are three types of conditional sentences.

    - Conditional 1 refers to an event in the present or the near future that is likely to happen:

        If you give me her email address, I'll email her.

    - Conditional 2 refers to an event that is not likely to occur in the present or near future:

        If I won the English prize, I would spend my prize money on books.

        If we had air conditioning, we would not feel so hot and tired in the mornings.

    - Conditional 3 refers to an event that could have occurred in the past, but did not. The speaker wants to express a different outcome which could have happened:

        If he had checked his tires, he would have avoided the accident.

    Here, the speaker did not check his tires so a tire exploded and he crashed the car.

EXERCISE 1

Fill in the blanks with the past perfect tense of the verbs in parentheses.

After I _____ (already, make) dinner, my roommate set the table.

After I **had already made** dinner, my roommate set the table.

1. I was excited to leave on vacation. I _____ (just, finish) packing.

2. Lina was late. By the time she arrived, the party _____ (already, started)

3. I saw my sister yesterday. I _____ (not, see) her in a week.

4. By the time my daughter came home last night, I _____ (go) to bed.

5. After the train _____ (already, leave) the station, the conductor realized the keys were missing.

EXERCISE 2

Match a clause from the first column with one from the second column. Look at the example to help you.

When the teacher arrived at the classroom,	when Sue called her.
Had the children eaten their lunch	when the doorbell rang.
Anita had already heard the news	when the alarm rang?
When the fire department arrived,	the students had left.
Samuel had just finished breakfast	because she had lost weight.
I didn't recognize Bonnie	the house had already burned to the ground.

EXERCISE 3

The following sentences mention a probable or possible situation. Fill in the blanks with the correct form of the verbs in parentheses.

If it **is not** (not, be) cold today, I **will go** (go) swimming.

1. I _____ (take) the dog for a walk if I _____ (not, jog) in the park.

2. If the class _____ (complete) the assignment, the teacher _____ (let) them leave early.

3. The mechanic _____ (not, repair) the car if the part _____ (not, arrive).

4. She _____ (bake) a cake if she _____ (have) enough time.

5. If you _____ (not, let) the dog into the house, it _____ (not, stop) barking.

EXERCISE 4

Unscramble the following groups of words, and make them into sentences or questions that describe an unlikely or impossible situation. Do not add or delete any words. Pay attention to punctuation.

to the gym / if she had / she would go / enough time

If she had enough time, she would go to the gym.

1. the extra weight / if he exercised / he would lose / every day

2. him / if you gave / to the interview / your car? / would he drive

3. the homework / if they did / better / grammar / they would understand

4. this one? / if Amy found / would she quit / another job

5. in our lives / if we retired / less stress / we would have / in the country

EXERCISE 5

The following sentences mention impossible conditions referring to past events that cannot be changed. <u>Underline</u> the correct verb tense in parentheses.

If I had wanted to talk to her, I (will call, would call, **would have called**) her.

If I had wanted to talk to her, I **would have called** her.

1. We would have left on time if it (does not snow, did not snow, **had not snowed**).

2. If she had been more polite to her customers, they (will leave, would leave, **would have left**) a bigger tip.

3. I (will reply, would reply, **would have replied**) to your email if my computer had not crashed.

Part 2 Review

Self-Study

PART 2

7 COMBINING CLAUSES

8 PRESENT PERFECT

9 MODALS

10 TYPES OF QUESTIONS AND SHORT ANSWERS

11 PREPOSITIONS AND PHRASAL VERBS

12 PAST PERFECT AND CONDITIONALS

OVERVIEW

The self-assessments in this unit give you a chance to review and reinforce the grammar points from Part 2 (Chapters 7–12). Check your knowledge and if you find areas that need more attention, go back to the appropriate chapter and review the material.

EXERCISE 1

Clauses are parts of sentences that contain a subject and a verb. They can be connected with connecting words. Choose the best connecting word from the following list to connect the clauses below.

who	or	while	whose	but

1. The cheque arrived, _____ it was already too late.

2. Music was playing in the background _____ they were eating.

3. This is the man _____ shoes are in the corridor.

4. We could order in a pizza, _____ we could go to a restaurant.

5. They are the students _____ passed the exam.

EXERCISE 2

Choose the best conjunction (*for, and, nor, but, or, yet, so*) or conjunctive adverb (*therefore, however, whereas, furthermore, moreover*, etc.) to connect or rephrase the following sentences. There may be more than one possible answer.

The photograph is old and in black and white. Their faces are still quite clear.

The photograph is old and in black and white, but their faces are still quite clear.

The photograph is old and in black and white; however, their faces are still quite clear.

1. Spring is early this year. The flowers haven't blossomed yet.

   _____

2. I don't have enough money to pay you right now. I can write a cheque.

   _____

3. I brought salad. I brought dessert.

   _____

4. Monica received a diamond ring from her fiancé. It turned out to be glass.

   _____

5. I was late for the concert. I snuck in quietly through the back door.

   _____

EXERCISE 3

To review some irregular verb forms, fill in the chart for the simple past and the past participle for the following verbs.

Verb	Simple Past	Past Participle
become		
	got	
		kept
	quit	
see		
take		

EXERCISE 4

The present perfect is used to indicate an indefinite past or an action that started in the past and continues to the present. Fill in the blanks with the correct form of the present perfect tense of the verbs in parentheses.

Joanna _____ (be) a dance instructor for most of her life. She started to dance at the age of five and _____ (stop [negative]) ever since. For many years she studied ballet and jazz, but her real passion was in ballroom dancing. She studied ballroom dancing immediately after middle school. She was first asked to teach when she was only 16. Although she is much younger than some of her students, she _____ (let, never) age get in the way of her passion. She teaches her students the same passion, especially the very young and the older generation that need some encouragement. She _____ (work) at the national school of dance for several years now and she _____ (win) many contests and awards. She will continue to share her passion for dance for many more good years to come.

EXERCISE 5

Fill in the blanks with the correct form of the verbs in parentheses. Choose from the present perfect or the simple past.

1. Roxanna and Gustav _____ (be) married for 15 years.

2. Roxanna _____ (work) as an architect for many years before she quit her job.

3. She _____ (write) many articles in the national architectural magazines.

4. Her husband Gustav works for the local library. He gets very proud when he finds his wife's articles in the magazines. He _____ (always, encourage) his wife to write more articles.

5. The first time Roxanna's article was published, Gustav _____ (send) a dozen red roses to her office.

EXERCISE 6

The present perfect progressive is almost always interchangeable with the present perfect, but it has a more immediate and sometimes more intense feel to the verb. Change the following present perfect verbs to the present perfect progressive. Look at the example to help you.

Present Perfect	Present Perfect Progressive
I have talked for two hours.	I have been talking for two hours.
She has lived here for a long time.	
We have cleaned this garage all day.	
It hasn't rained all summer.	

EXERCISE 7

Modals are auxiliaries used to create a sense of ability, necessity, advice, or preference. Modals can also be used for polite requests and offers. Fill in each blank below with the correct modal from the following list. You may use each modal more than once, and there may be more than one correct answer.

| would | could | should | may | might | can | will | must | have to | ought to |

1. _____ you please open the door for me? My hands are full.

2. Where _____ I put your boxes?

3. The doctor insisted that you _____ take your medication before breakfast.

4. If your driver's test is next month, you _____ practise more often.

5. _____ we go now? It seems everyone is ready.

6. When she was six years old, she _____ speak three languages.

7. She has forgotten how to speak Portuguese, so now she _____ only speak two languages.

8. Don't forget! You _____ return your books to the library today.

9. The weather channel said it _____ snow tonight; there's only a 40 percent chance.

10. _____ you give me a hand with these grocery bags? Thank you.

EXERCISE 8

Turn each sentence below into an information question using one of the following question words. The information you want to ask about is **bolded** and underlined.

what	when	how	why	how far	how long	where

My wallet is in **my pocket**.

Where is your wallet?

1. It has been raining **all afternoon**.

   _____

2. The train arrives **at midnight**.

   _____

3. **He** was giving a lecture on retirement.

   _____

4. She didn't get the flowers **because the sender had the wrong address**.

   _____

5. The children are eating **candies**.

   _____

EXERCISE 9

Yes / no (interrogative) questions are formed to receive either a yes or a no response. Change each of the following sentences into a yes / no question.

The game started. → Did the game start?

1. They should arrive here on time.

   _____

2. It has been raining all week.

_____

3. The students are studying for the exam.

_____

4. The doctor was examining his patients.

_____

5. I will see you tomorrow.

_____

EXERCISE 10

Short answers are used for quick replies. Fill in the following chart with both a positive and a negative short answer. Look at the example to help you.

Question	Positive Short Answer	Negative Short Answer
Does she have a bike?	Yes, she does.	No, she doesn't.
Was it cold outside?		
Should we leave now?		
Has he left yet?		
Will you call me?		

EXERCISE 11

Change the following positive questions to negative questions. Use the example to help you.

Positive Question	Negative Question
Did he get a scholarship?	Didn't he get a scholarship?
Does she eat well every day?	
Have you been up all night?	
Could he do this favour for me?	
Will she write me a letter?	

EXERCISE 12

Tag questions are asked when we need confirmation of something we think is true. Tag the following statements. Look at the example to help you.

Statement	Verb Tense	Statement + Tag Question
They are ready.	simple present	They are ready, aren't they?
It was expensive.	simple past	
She'll go to India one day.	future with *will*	
It's going to snow.	future with *be going to*	
We are watching it now.	present progressive	
They were eating.	past progressive	
You have finished your meal.	present perfect	

EXERCISE 13

Prepositions give information about time and space. Fill in the blanks in the following sentences with the correct prepositions. Use the words from the list. Use each word only once.

| in |
| on |
| about |
| inside |
| next to |

1. Stick the label _____ top of the box, so we can see it.

2. I wonder what's _____ this gift bag.

3. My friends always want to sit _____ me in class.

4. The twins were born _____ the month of May.

5. Everyone should get here _____ six o'clock or so.

EXERCISE 14

A phrasal verb is a two-word or three-word verb that has its own unique meaning. Fill in the blanks in the first column with the correct phrasal verb from the second column.

Sentence	Phrasal Verb
Don't forget to _____ any new words in the dictionary.	take off
My neighbour wants me to _____ her cat while she's away.	put on
The planes _____ every 40 minutes.	get down
_____ from that tree! It's dangerous.	run out of
We've _____ milk.	look after
It's cold outside. You should _____ a scarf and gloves.	look up

EXERCISE 15

The past perfect is the verb tense that indicates a past action / event that occurred before a more recent past action / event. Read the following paragraph and (circle) the correct verb tense(s) in each sentence. Then decide: what do you think happened to Jill and Rob?

Last spring, Jill and Rob (drove / had driven) to Florida for March break. They (never drove / had never driven) there before; in the past, they (always took / had always taken) a plane. This year, they (decided / had decided) to take their car.

They (set off / had set off) at 5:00 AM on Friday morning. Rob (packed / had packed) a cooler with sandwiches and muffins, and Jill (made / had made) a thermos of coffee. They drove to the US border, but they (had to / had had to) wait there for two hours. Many other people (made / had made) the same decision to leave early in the morning, and the border (was / had been) busy.

Eventually, they (entered / had entered) the United States. However, they (drove / had driven) only 160 kilometres when something terrible (happened / had happened) . . .

EXERCISE 16

Conditional 1 is used to refer to a probable or possible situation. Conditional 2 refers to an unlikely event in the future. Conditional 3 refers to a past event that cannot be changed. Identify the number of the condition on the blank line provided and then fill in the blanks with the correct tense of the verbs in parentheses.

1   If it is sunny, we **will play** (play) soccer outdoors.

2   If she called me, I **would help** (help) her gladly.

3   If we **had arrived** (arrive) sooner, we would have caught the earlier bus.

1. _____   She would pay the rent if she _____ (have) the money.

2. _____   If I get the letter tomorrow, I _____ (let) you know.

3. _____   He would have been accepted to the basketball team if he _____ (be) five inches taller.

4. _____   It will get here if the mail strike _____ (end).

APPENDIX A: COMMON IRREGULAR VERBS

Base Form	Simple Past	Past Participle	Base Form	Simple Past	Past Participle
arise	arose	arisen	go	went	gone
be	was, were	been	grind	ground	ground
beat	beat	beaten	grow	grew	grown
become	became	become	hang	hung	hung
begin	began	begun	have	had	had
bend	bent	bent	hear	heard	heard
bet	bet	bet	hide	hid	hidden
bind	bound	bound	hit	hit	hit
bite	bit	bitten	hold	held	held
bleed	bled	bled	hurt	hurt	hurt
blow	blew	blown	keep	kept	kept
break	broke	broken	kneel	knelt	knelt
bring	brought	brought	know	knew	known
build	built	built	lay	laid	laid
burst	burst	burst	lead	led	led
buy	bought	bought	leave	left	left
catch	caught	caught	lend	lent	lent
choose	chose	chosen	let	let	let
come	came	come	lie	lay	lain
cost	cost	cost	lose	lost	lost
cut	cut	cut	make	made	made
deal	dealt	dealt	mean	meant	meant
dig	dug	dug	meet	met	met
do	did	done	mistake	mistook	mistaken
draw	drew	drawn	pay	paid	paid
drink	drank	drunk	put	put	put
drive	drove	driven	prove	proved	proven / proved
eat	ate	eaten	quit	quit	quit
fall	fell	fallen	read	read	read
feed	fed	fed	ride	rode	ridden
feel	felt	felt	ring	rang	rung
fight	fought	fought	rise	rose	risen
find	found	found	run	ran	run
fly	flew	flown	say	said	said
forbid	forbade	forbidden	see	saw	seen
forget	forgot	forgotten	sell	sold	sold
forgive	forgave	forgiven	send	sent	sent
freeze	froze	frozen	set	set	set
get	got	gotten	shake	shook	shaken
give	gave	given	shine	shone	shone

Base Form	Simple Past	Past Participle
shoot	shot	shot
show	showed	shown
shrink	shrank	shrunk
shut	shut	shut
sing	sang	sung
sink	sank	sunk
sit	sat	sat
sleep	slept	slept
slide	slid	slid
speak	spoke	spoken
speed	sped	sped
spend	spent	spent
spin	spun	spun
split	split	split
spread	spread	spread
spring	sprang	sprung
stand	stood	stood
steal	stole	stolen
stick	stuck	stuck
sting	stung	stung

Base Form	Simple Past	Past Participle
stink	stank	stunk
strike	struck	struck
swear	swore	sworn
sweep	swept	swept
swim	swam	swum
swing	swung	swung
take	took	taken
teach	taught	taught
tear	tore	torn
tell	told	told
think	thought	thought
throw	threw	thrown
understand	understood	understood
upset	upset	upset
wake	woke	woken
wear	wore	worn
win	won	won
wind	wound	wound
withdraw	withdrew	withdrawn
write	wrote	written

APPENDIX B: CONJUNCTIVE ADVERBS

Conjunctive adverbs are used at the beginning of sentences or clauses. We use conjunctive adverbs to show the connection between the sentence or clause they introduce and the information that came immediately before. Remember that before a conjunctive adverb, you need either a period (.) or a semi-colon (;). After a conjunctive adverb, you need a comma (,).

Conjunctive Adverb	Purpose	Example Sentences
in addition	to give more information	Chris volunteers at the art gallery; **in addition,** he is captain of the basketball team. Pollution in the river has lowered the fish population; **in addition,** it has killed plant life.
furthermore		The new mayor will lower taxes; **furthermore,** she will improve health services. Research into ghosts is a waste of time; **furthermore,** it's a waste of money.
moreover		The castle is a historical landmark; **moreover,** it's a popular tourist attraction. Small houses are cute; **moreover,** they are easy to keep clean.
besides		The Grand Hotel is too expensive; **besides,** it's too far away. Sociology 101 is not useful to my career; **besides,** it's boring!
for example	to give an example	Today's teenagers have many more gadgets than their parents did; **for example,** they have iPads and smartphones. Thai food is delicious; **for example,** Thai green curry is a tasty dish.
for instance		Why don't you take a language course? **For instance,** you could take Spanish or Russian. Hypnosis is often used to treat addictions; **for instance,** it is helpful for nicotine or alcohol addiction.
therefore	to show a result	We lost our semi-final match; **therefore,** we will not be in the final. Liz is allergic to cheese; **therefore,** she cannot eat pizza.
however	to show something unexpected	I thought I had done badly on the test; **however,** I got 85 percent! The weather forecast predicted rain; **however,** it was a nice, sunny day.
on the other hand	to show a contrast	The red coat is more stylish; **on the other hand,** the blue coat is warmer. The leather chair is more comfortable; **on the other hand,** the wooden chair is cheaper.
in contrast		Canada has very cold winters; **in contrast,** Arizona has warm and sunny winters. Susannah is good at science; **in contrast,** her brother Stuart is an excellent artist and musician.
in fact	to show emphasis	Nelson Mandela was a great leader; **in fact,** he was a hero to many people. Jenna is a good singer; **in fact,** she is the best singer in her choir.
actually	to correct someone	People sometimes say Ying is unfriendly; **actually,** she is just very shy. Some people think dragons are real animals; **actually,** they just appear in stories.

APPENDIX C: SUBORDINATING CONJUNCTIONS

We use subordinating conjunctions to connect dependent clauses to independent clauses. The order of the sentence can be IC + conjunction + DC, or it can be conjunction + DC + comma + IC.

The school bus is cancelled **whenever** it snows.

Whenever it snows, the school bus is cancelled.

Subordinating Conjunction	Purpose	Example Sentences
before after when whenever while until as soon as	to show a time relationship	Turn off the lights **before** you go to bed. **Before** you go to bed, turn off the lights. Jake backpacked in Europe **after** he graduated. **After** he graduated, Jake backpacked in Europe. They will text me **when** they are at the theatre. **When** they are at the theatre, they will text me. My basement floods **whenever** it rains. **Whenever** it rains, my basement floods. Mia hit a deer **while** she was driving home. **While** she was driving home, Mia hit a deer. You should stay here **until** you hear from him. **Until** you hear from him, you should stay here. I knew the news was bad **as soon as** I saw her face. **As soon as** I saw her face, I knew the news was bad.
so (that)	to show a purpose	Ami bought a cookbook **so (that)** she could learn to cook. **So (that)** she could learn to cook, Ami bought a cookbook.
because as	to show a reason	We're happy **because** it's Friday. **Because** it's Friday, we're happy. There is no school tomorrow **as** it's Canada Day. **As** it's Canada Day, there is no school tomorrow.
whereas while	to show a contrast	Biology 100 is easy, **whereas** Chemistry 101 is hard. **Whereas** Chemistry 101 is hard, Biology 100 is easy. China is a large country, **while** Singapore is small. **While** Singapore is a small country, China is large.
although even though	to show an unexpected event	Our flight is on time **although** it's foggy. **Although** it's foggy, our flight is on time. My plants died **even though** I watered them. **Even though** I watered my plants, they died.
if even if unless	to show a condition	We'll get a puppy **if** you promise to take care of it. **If** you promise to take care of it, we'll get a puppy. They won't make the playoffs, **even if** they win today. **Even if** they win today, they won't make the playoffs. We can't go skiing **unless** it snows tonight. **Unless** it snows tonight, we can't go skiing.

APPENDIX D: PHRASAL VERBS

Phrasal Verb	Example Sentence
break down	Our car **broke down** on the highway to Vancouver.
break up	I have sad news. Betsy and Roy have **broken up**.
bring up	The staff **brought up** some important points at the meeting.
call off	If she doesn't feel better by Saturday, we'll have to **call off** the party.
catch up on	He has to stay late and **catch up on** his work.
catch up with	You go on ahead. We'll **catch up with** you.
check out	There's a new bar in town; let's **check** it **out**.
come across	I don't know this word. I've never **come across** it before.
come back	When you **come back** to Canada, we'll go out for dinner.
fall through	Kai and I had planned to go backpacking, but our plans **fell through**.
fill out	To apply for a passport, you need to **fill out** some forms.
get along with	Ben didn't **get along with** his sister when they were children.
get behind in	Don't **get behind in** your work; it will be hard to catch up later.
get down	Children! **Get down** from that tree! You'll fall!
get in	Did you have a good time last night? What time did you **get in**?
get off	**Get off** the bus at River Street, then walk for 500 metres.
get on	Don't be afraid to **get on** the horse; it won't hurt you.
get out of	I have a previous commitment, but I can try to **get out of** it.
get over	It's taking me a long time to **get over** this cold.
get together	Shall we **get together** on the weekend and have coffee?
get up	I always **get up** at 6:00 in the morning.
give away	We **gave away** a lot of furniture when we moved to a smaller house.
give up	Meg worked hard to reach her goals; she never **gave up**.
go away	There's a strange dog in our front yard. I'll tell him to **go away**.
go over	Let's meet on the weekend and **go over** our travel plans.
grow up	The children are **growing up** so quickly!
keep on	We told them to be quiet, but they **kept on** singing and shouting.
leave out	When you write your essay, don't **leave out** that reference.
let down	Hannah promised to help me, but she **let** me **down**.
look away	She can't stand horror movies; she always **looks away**.
look after	My grandparents **looked after** me when I was a child.
look down on	Don't **look down on** me just because I am not good at math!
look for	I spend too much time **looking for** my glasses.
look forward to	The students are **looking forward to** the ski trip.
look in on	I **look in on** my children before I go to bed.
look out	When you're driving in the city, **look out** for cyclists.
look up	I don't know the capital of Nigeria. I'll **look** it **up**.
look up to	His children all admire him and **look up to** him.
make out	I can't **make out** what that street sign says. Can you read it?
make up (1)	Even as a young child, she loved to **make up** stories and poems.

Phrasal Verb	Example Sentence
make up (2)	If you miss the test, you can **make** it **up** at a later date.
make up (3)	I'm sorry we had an argument. Let's **make up** and be friends again.
pick up (1)	Don't drop garbage on the floor. Please **pick** it **up**.
pick up (2)	I'll **pick** you **up** in my car at a quarter to nine.
pick up (3)	Karen didn't take Chinese lessons, but she **picked up** some phrases.
point out	If you see George, please **point** him **out** to me.
put away	If you use my iPad charger, please **put** it **away** afterwards.
put down	That's a valuable piece of glass; you should **put** it **down**.
put off (1)	I need to see a dentist. I can't **put** it **off** any longer.
put off (2)	Don't let him **put** you **off**—you should apply for the job!
put on (1)	We're having dinner with Grandmother. **Put on** a nice skirt.
put on (2)	They aren't angry. They're **putting** it **on** to make you feel bad.
put out	Please **put out** your cigarette; you can't smoke here.
put up with	I'm not going to **put up with** his rudeness anymore!
run away	We used to have a small cat, but he **ran away**.
rule out	The house burned to the ground. The police have not **ruled out** arson.
run out of	I'm always **running out of** money! I need a part-time job.
see about	I'm meeting my professor to **see about** getting an extension.
show up	We invited Mike for dinner, but he didn't **show up**.
take after	The girl **takes after** her mother in appearance and personality.
take back	If you don't like your new TV set, **take** it **back** to the store.
take down	After the holidays, we'll have to **take down** the decorations.
take in (1)	She's lost weight, so she needs to **take in** all her clothes.
take in (2)	There was a stray cat in my neighbourhood, so I **took** him **in**.
take off (1)	The plane **takes off** at 3:15 and lands at 8:20.
take off (2)	If you're hot, why don't you **take off** your sweater?
take on	Roger has agreed to **take on** the organization of the project.
take up (1)	We never see Gerry, now that he's **taken up** golf.
take up (2)	Are we going to **take up** the answers in class tomorrow?
throw out	I'm so mad! My roommate **threw out** my important letter.
try on	This dress is pretty. Why don't you **try** it **on**?
turn down (1)	Henry was offered a job in Ottawa, but he **turned** it **down**.
turn down (2)	I can't stand this music! Can you **turn** it **down**, please?
turn off	We're going out. Let's **turn off** the television.
turn on	I can't **turn on** my computer—I hope it isn't broken.
turn up	**Turn up** the radio; I love this song!
write down	**Write** this information **down**, so you don't forget it.

GLOSSARY

Word or Term	Definition	Chapter	Page
absent-minded	forgetful	11	221
accessible	able to be reached or connected	6	114
accomplishment	an achievement	5	92
account for	explain	12	239
accountability	a state of being responsible to someone	12	239
achieve	gain something through hard work	1	15
acquaintance	someone with whom you are friendly, but whom you don't know well	7	144
addiction	a physical need for a substance such as tobacco, alcohol, coffee	10	203
adrenaline rush	a sudden burst of excitement	2	34
alien	a creature from outer space, an extraterrestrial	9	184
architect	a person who designs buildings	3	54
arena	a big place for an activity such as sports	5	92
attic	a small room in the top part of a house, under the roof	2	34
backpack (v.)	travel with a backpack, usually cheaply and for a long period of time	4	71
backslide	return to bad habits or bad ways	12	239
bilingualism	an ability to speak two languages	1	15
capture	catch	8	162
cautious	careful	9	184
cellar	a room underneath a house, often used for storage	2	34
cherished (adj.)	precious, much-loved	11	221
cold turkey (adv.)	all at once, not gradually	10	203
concept	an idea or thought	12	239
counterpart	someone with a similar role, somewhere else	5	91
criticize	make negative comments about	5	92
curiosity	an interest in finding out something	2	34
dynamic	full of life and energy	5	92
effective	giving the desired result	1	15
emphasize	draw particular attention to	5	92
encourage	support someone in doing something	5	92
encouragement	emotional support and confidence given by one person to another	1	15
endurance	the ability to continue to carry out a task over a long period of time	8	162
enforce	make something happen using power or force	1	15
engrave	cut words or a design into metal or wood	2	35
enthusiastic	interested and excited by something	4	71
erode	become worn away over time such as by wind or other weather conditions	3	55
evolve	develop and change over time	7	143
exotic	from a faraway place or a culturally different place	7	143
expectation	a vision of what should be achieved or done	5	92
fluid	liquid	10	203
goofy	silly	11	222
hostel	cheap accommodation, often for backpackers	4	72
hypnosis	mental state of being in a trance	10	203
illegible	impossible to read	4	72
inappropriate	not good or acceptable for the circumstance or place	5	92
inkling	a feeling about something	11	221

Word or Term	Definition	Chapter	Page
inspire	give someone ideas for creative work	3	55
intensify	become stronger	5	92
invisible	impossible to see	10	203
maintain	keep in good condition	3	55
mansion	a very large and possibly luxurious house	3	55
means (n.)	financial ability	6	114
meditation	deep thinking, often in a religious setting	8	162
mesmerize	hold someone's attention; put someone in a state of hypnosis	2, 10	34, 203
messy	not organized; untidy	11	221
official	connected with the government or other authority	1	14
opportunity	a chance to do exciting things	5	92
optimistic	having a positive outlook or opinion	6	114
orphan	a child without parents	3	54
outrageous	out of the ordinary, shocking	8	162
pace (v.)	walk in continuous steps, often back and forth, while thinking	11	222
panic	sudden fear, sometimes irrational	11	222
patience	the ability to wait without being nervous or anxious	2	34
phobia	an irrational and uncontrollable fear of something	10	203
pile (n.)	a stack of flat objects on top of each other	11	221
professional (adj.)	doing something as a job, not as a hobby	4	72
purchase	buy	3	54
quality	how good or valuable something is	7	143
quantity	the number or amount of something	7	143
real-estate agent	a person who helps you to buy or sell a house	3	54
reminisce	remember happily	4	72
rerun (n.)	a television program repeated from past seasons	9	184
researcher	a person who carries out academic studies	1	15
retirement	terminating your profession due to being older (e.g., 65 years of age)	3	54
schedule (n.)	a formal plan stating when things must happen (e.g., with transportation)	4	71
seal (v.)	close off	2	35
shrug	raise the shoulders in a gesture to say, "I don't know" or "I don't understand"	4	72
sibling	a brother or sister	11	222
sigh of relief	a breath taken after learning that there is no longer a need for fear	11	222
simultaneously	at the same time	8	162
sitcom	a situation comedy: a television program based on funny everyday events	9	184
skeptical	having doubts about the existence or effectiveness of something	10	203
social network	an online social site like Facebook or Twitter	7	143
sound barrier	the point at which the speed of a spacecraft is the same as the speed of sound	6	114
stamina	the ability to do something physical for a long time	5	92
stunning (adj.)	extremely beautiful	6	114
support (n.)	emotional or financial help	1	15
sustain	suffer (e.g., an injury)	5	92
Swiss ball	a big, soft ball, often used in physical exercise	8	162
trance	in a half sleep or conscious state, hypnotized	10	203
transgression	an act that is socially unacceptable or unlawful	12	239
unforgettable	always remembered	6	114
viable	able to live or survive	5	92
withered	dried up, aged, looking old	2	34